CAKE ANGELS

JULIA THOMAS

Collins

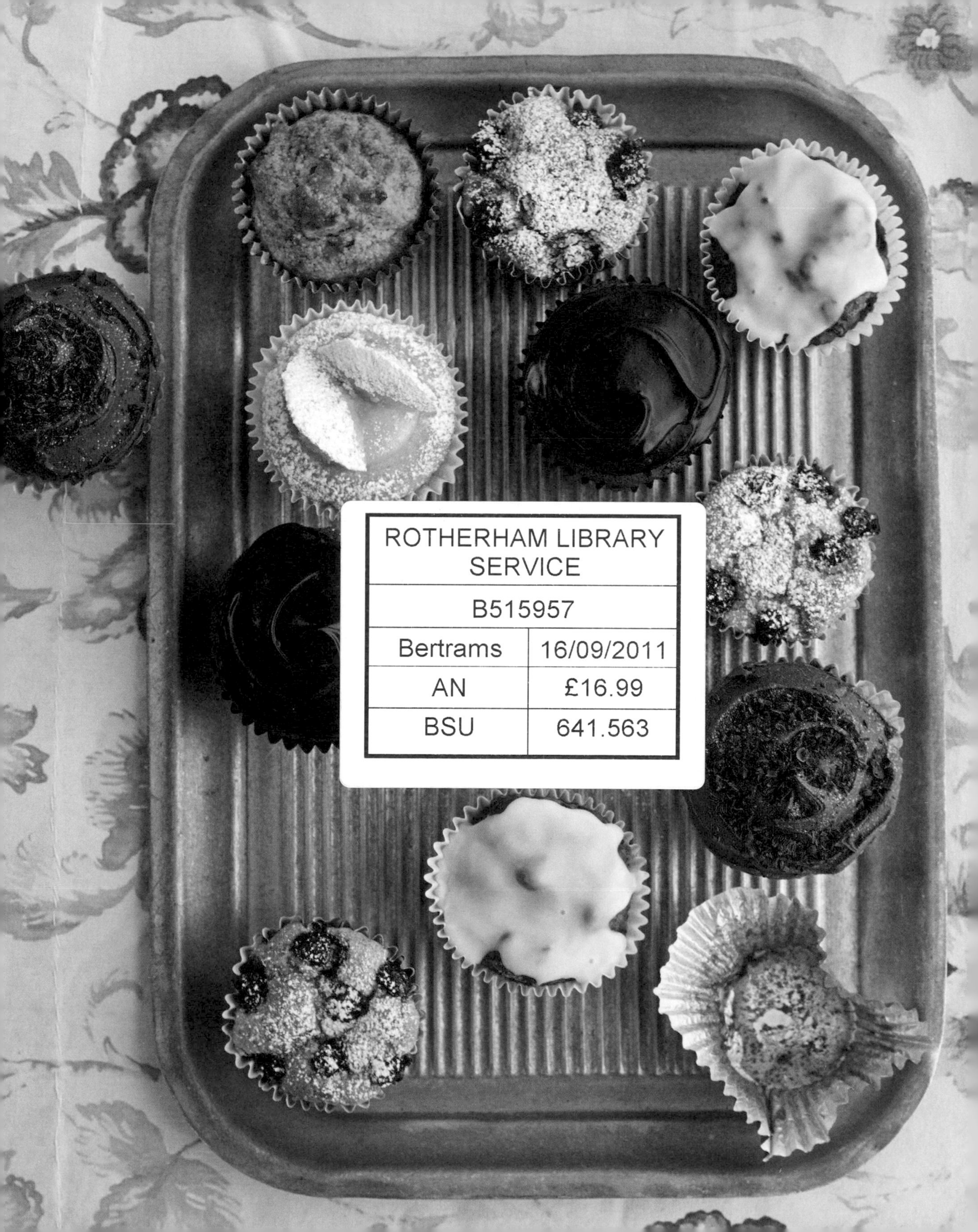

Contents

Introduction

Take a moment to close your eyes and imagine that wonderfully evocative smell of a freshly baked cake, and then imagine slowly sinking your teeth into all its glorious, gorgeous gooeyness – bliss. There really isn't anything more satisfyingly indulgent than baking your very own cake, something just for you (and perhaps a friend or two). However, many people have been missing out on this pleasure in the belief that dairy-, wheat- and gluten-free cakes are difficult to make successfully. I don't know why because as I have discovered over the past few years, this is so far from the truth. Baking without dairy, wheat and gluten really is straightforward and in this book I hope to show you how to bake really delicious and beautiful cakes. And all my recipes work equally well using butter and normal plain and self-raising flours; just remember to remove the xanthan gum from your list of ingredients.

Little did I imagine as a child standing on a stool, helping my mother bake one of her delicious cakes, that one day I would be an award-winning artisan baker, baking on television for Michelin-starred chefs and princesses, both real and self-appointed! My journey from child enthusiast to bespoke baker has not been a conventional one, but if you dream of yummy cakes like I do, it's amazing where your dreams can take you. I have always loved cake: light delicate sponges, rich moist fruit cakes, spicy carrot cakes and dense chocolaty delights. In fact, any cake is guaranteed to put a twinkle in my eye and a huge smile on my face. The wonderful smell of a baking cake can still take me back to that happy and carefree time with my mother and now when I bake, my young son stands next to me, determined to help and even more determined to lick the bowl!

In early 2004, whilst pregnant with my first longed-for child, I was diagnosed with an aggressive form of breast cancer that had already spread to my lymph nodes. I had to make the mental shift from excited mum-to-be to anxiously discussing life-saving treatment options with my surgeon and oncologist. I won't pretend it was easy because it wasn't. My oncologist was brilliant and came up with a plan of action to work around my pregnancy. I couldn't have the standard cocktail of drugs because no one knew what effect they could have on my baby, so a special regime was designed for me. I underwent four courses of chemotherapy before giving birth to my son and a further four immediately after the birth. Two weeks after finishing my chemotherapy, I had the first of 17 radiotherapy sessions, which once completed were immediately replaced with a year's course of the drug Herceptin. I was exhausted, physically and emotionally, but luckily Charlie was a really good baby and my husband was amazingly supportive. Everyone has their own way of coping with a life-threatening diagnosis and mine was to try and help myself by looking at alternative ways of treating cancer which would complement the conventional treatments I was having. So after hours of research and lengthy discussions with a nutritionist, I made a life-changing decision to radically change my diet and eliminate all dairy products, milk, cheese, butter and yoghurt. Whilst I never doubted changing my diet was worth it, I was devastated that I couldn't just pop to the bakers to cheer myself up with a delicious cake. After all, when you are miserable, treating yourself to something yummy is usually a good way of lifting your spirits.

In desperation, I scoured bakeries, supermarkets and upmarket health food shops for suitably delicious dairy-free cakes. Whilst I found a few, none of them satisfied my need for something wickedly sinful, beautiful to look at and tasting like normal cake. Some people would gracefully accept the situation and resign themselves to a life without, but not me. As far as I'm concerned, 'Where there is a will, there is a way' and I thought, why not bake my own, so I did. Nothing was too complicated or too daunting. If I felt like eating it, I baked it, and it was brilliant. I experimented with dairy-free alternatives and adapted many of my mother's recipes, most of which were successful. I can't begin to tell you how good it felt to sink my teeth into something sweet, sticky and totally delicious, but it was very close to heavenly! From that point on, I always took my own cakes with me wherever I went. After all, I didn't want to miss out, and it wasn't long before people were waiting for me to arrive! A friend then asked if I would consider baking wheat- and gluten-free cakes, as her young son was intolerant of both. Loving a challenge, I said I would give it a go. I was so pleased with the results that wheat and gluten joined dairy in being banished from my kitchen forever.

Whilst I was conducting my culinary research, I couldn't help thinking, surely I am not alone in this quest? There must be others out there, just like me, yearning for luscious cakes. And I was right. I discovered between 20% and 30% of the UK population believes it has an intolerance, whilst between 1% and 2% of the population has a diagnosed allergy. Recent evidence also suggests that 1 in 100 people is affected by coeliac disease, so there are lots and lots of people out there like me searching for that 'Holy Grail'– the cake 'you can have and eat'. So with my health improving, I decided to launch my own bespoke baking service, Cake Angels. Rather than taking on the responsibilities and ties of a shop, I decided I would bake a range of cakes to order and dispatch them by overnight courier, meaning they could be out of the oven and on a customer's doorstep within 24 hours. It didn't take long for word to get out and my belief that people on restricted diets were badly served when it came to simple, yet beautifully delicious, cakes was proved to be right. Soon I was baking non-stop and not just for customers with allergies or intolerances, but for people who have simply made a lifestyle choice not to eat animal fats, wheat and highly processed foods and, of course, for anyone who just loves cake. A few months later, my dairy-, wheat- and gluten-free brownies won a coveted two gold stars at The Guild of Fine Food Great Taste Awards, with the judges commenting that they were exquisite – no mean feat considering I was competing with products containing dairy! Subsequently, numerous articles about Cake Angels have appeared in the press and interest and demand continues to increase as more and more people realize how delicious dairy-, wheat- and gluten-free foods can be.

Many of my customers have shared with me their stories of disappointment and frustration with the limited and uninspiring range of products available to them, but are unsure of baking their own cakes. My cakes are not complicated to bake and I don't use unnecessarily baffling and inaccessible ingredients (in fact, most can be bought at the supermarket). Baking the simplest of cakes can fill your house with delicious smells and fresh out of the oven, they taste absolutely gorgeous. My book is full of my favourite recipes and will show you how easy it is to bake gloriously moist and delicious dairy-, wheat- and gluten- free cakes. Just follow my guidelines and tips and I guarantee you won't be disappointed.

Key Ingredients

Baking successfully with dairy-, wheat- and gluten-free ingredients is not as difficult as you may think and in most cases you use the same ingredients as you would in normal baking. There are, however, a few specialist ingredients that you need to make friends with, most of which can now be purchased from all the main supermarkets and good high street health food shops. This section contains information about the alternative ingredients that I use, as well as the ones you may already have lurking in the back of your cupboard.

Fats

Not only are they low in unsaturated fats, but dairy-free spreads can be used straight from the fridge, so you don't need to remember to take them out of the fridge to warm to room temperature.

* Dairy-free sunflower spread is what I use in most of my baking. It is not only free of dairy, but also GM ingredients, hydrogenated oils, artificial additives, emulsifiers, soya and gluten and has 70% less saturated fat than butter. I use Pure Sunflower, but a number of the big supermarkets have their own brand of 'free from' spreads. Always remember to check the ingredients label to be sure.

* Soya spread is also great for baking. It contains 59% vegetable oils and is also free from dairy, GM ingredients, hydrogenated oils, artificial additives, emulsifiers and gluten. It really is down to personal preference as to which type of spread you decide to use.

* Oils such as naturally refined sunflower and vegetable oils are wonderful to bake with, and I use organic oils in quite a few of my recipes. Other oils, such as hazelnut and walnut, are best used in very small quantities just to flavour.

* Coconut oil is hard and white at room temperature, but melts really easily and tastes wonderful. It is high in omega-3 fatty acids, essential amino acids and lauric acid and is stored in the body as energy, not fat. In fact, it is an all-round good guy. It is expensive, which is why I use it just for frostings. I use Biona Coconut Oil, which is available only from good health food shops or online at www.cakeangels.co.uk or www.naturallygoodfood.co.uk.

Milk

Dairy-free milks are really easy to bake with and can also be used to create authentic creams, frostings and curds. They are low in fat and are normally calcium-enriched, but check the ingredients label first.

* Liquid milks, such as soya, rice, almond and oat, are all great to bake with, but I find unsweetened soya milk, with its creamier texture and taste, is best for making creams and some frostings. All can be bought from the main supermarkets.

* Coconut milk has about 17% fat and is usually bought in cans from supermarkets. However, you can now buy a less creamy, low-fat coconut milk, which is similar to rice milk in texture and is sold in cartons at good health food shops.

* Soya double cream, also often referred to as whipping cream, is a blend of vegetable fats and hulled soya beans and is great for baking with. There are two brands available in this country: Granovita Organic CremoVita and Soyatoo. Both brands can be purchased from good high street health food shops or online at www.cakeangels.co.uk, www.naturallygoodfood.co.uk and www.veganstore.co.uk.

* Dairy-free sour cream is a soya-based cream that works really well in baking and tastes delicious served on jacket potatoes and in dips. I use Tofutti Sour Supreme, which at the moment can be purchased at good high street health food shops and online at www.cakeangels.co.uk or www.goodnessdirect.co.uk

* Coconut cream, not to be confused with creamed coconut that is sold as a hard block, is sold in cartons and can be found in all the main supermarkets. It is similar in texture to double cream and when whisked into soft peaks with a little added icing sugar, tastes wonderful.

* Powdered or dried dairy-free milks are usually dried soya milk, though if you prefer you can get dried almond milk. Both are quite expensive, but ideal to keep in your store cupboard. Neither is available in supermarkets yet and they have to be purchased from good health food shops or online at www.cakeangels.co.uk or www.goodnessdirect.co.uk. Don't be tempted to try Cow & Gate's Infasoy – it doesn't work for baking!

Flour

Wheat- and gluten-free flours can now be bought as premixed bags in all the main supermarkets, which makes life a lot easier. I have developed all the recipes in this book using the award-winning Doves Farm flours, but there are other very good ones available from health food shops. For the recipes in this book, you will use self-raising and plain flour. It is important to use the type of flour stated in the recipe, as the wrong flour will drastically affect the appearance and texture of the finished cake. Do make sure you check the sell-by date on your flours, as they do deteriorate over time.

Xanthan Gum

The magic ingredient that makes wheat- and gluten-free cakes such a success. Without it, your cakes will fall apart in a crumbly mess, so omit at your peril! I use Doves Farm Xanthan Gum, which is gluten-free and found in all the main supermarkets. The wheat- and gluten-free flours already contain a small amount, but I have found that to get the best results with cakes you need to add a little extra. Follow my instructions and you won't go wrong.

Baking powder

Not all baking powders are gluten-free, so please check the ingredients label. I use Dr. Oetker Gluten-free Baking Powder, which can be bought at all the main supermarkets. Do make sure you check the sell-by date because baking powder, like flour, does deteriorate over time.

Bicarbonate of soda

Commonly found in recipes with strong spicy flavours, such as gingerbread and parkin, as it has a rather bitter taste. It works best with acid-forming ingredients such as lemon juice, black treacle and dairy-free buttermilk. Again, make sure you check the sell-by date as it does deteriorate over time.

Cocoa powder

A gluten-free and inexpensive ingredient in baking. I always sift it with other dry ingredients so it is evenly distributed, or mix it with liquid to make a paste. If you love the taste of dark bitter chocolate, then chose a cocoa powder such as Green & Black's. If you like a slightly lighter, sweeter taste, then Sainsbury's cocoa powder might be for you. Don't use drinking chocolate, as this contains dried milk.

Oats

Although oats do not contain gluten, some people may be sensitive to a similar protein called avenins. Many oat products can be contaminated with wheat or barley, so it is important to use only gluten-free oats, which can be found in Sainsbury's, Tesco and all good health food shops.

Sugars

I prefer to use unrefined sugars in my recipes, but because they are darker in colour, your cakes will be darker in appearance. Do feel free to experiment.

* Caster sugar is small-grained and blends well in sponges and meringues.

* Granulated sugar is much coarser in texture and can give cakes a gritty texture.

* Icing sugar is very fine in texture and is occasionally used in making pastry bases, but most commonly it is used to make frostings and icings.

* Muscovado sugars are made from raw cane sugar and vary in colour and taste. I use light muscovado sugar in a number of recipes because it provides a lovely light toffee flavour. Dark muscovado sugar works really well in gingerbread and parkin because it has a very strong molasses flavour.

* Demerara sugar has a lower molasses content with larger crystals and is great for sprinkling on top of cakes for a nice crunchy finish.

* Golden syrup and black treacle are made from crystallized sugar. I use both in my recipes.

* Honey has been used as a sweetener for centuries. I use runny honey in my recipes, as it dissolves much faster.

Condensed milk

Condensed milk is milk that has had half the water content removed and sugar added. Until recently this ingredient was out of bounds, but then I discovered I could make my own dairy-free version using dried soya milk. Yippee, I can now make thick caramel for Millionaire's Shortbread and my Chocolate Nutty Caramels – bliss.

Eggs

I use organic free-range eggs in all my recipes. I have indicated in each recipe whether to use large or medium eggs and it is important you follow the instructions because liquid content can affect the result of your cake.

Chocolate

My favourite ingredient! I always use organic dairy-, wheat- and gluten-free 60% dark, milk and white chocolate drops in my baking as they melt faster and are easier to use. You can now buy them direct from www.cakeangels.co.uk. You can also buy chocolate buttons in good health food shops and supermarkets but they are normally sold in small quantities and are expensive.

When decorating with chocolate I do use bars for curls or grating. You can buy bars of dairy-free chocolate in most good health food shops and all the main supermarkets stock Kinnerton's dairy-, wheat- and gluten-free chocolate bars, which you will find in the 'free from' food sections.

Instructions, Tips & Equipment

❧

Baking should be a real pleasure and not a chore and if you follow my recipes and tips, you will find that baking without dairy, wheat and gluten is no different to any other type of baking. I have spent some wonderfully exciting and frustrating hours in the kitchen experimenting and developing my recipes, so to help you avoid some of my mistakes, I have devised a few basic rules that you need to follow:

~

Make sure you have the correct ingredients

Always read a recipe through first

Follow my instructions

*Have fun. Cakes always look and taste better
if you have enjoyed yourself baking them*

~

Tips

My recipes include individual instructions for making the perfect cake. However, there are some general tips that will help you get the most out of baking:

* Always weigh your ingredients accurately.

* Take care when transferring cake mixture into a tin. Stiff mixtures need to be levelled and smoothed with a small dip in the middle to ensure a nice level surface once baked.

* When dividing the mixture into two or more tins, do so as evenly as possible. I weigh each tin and adjust accordingly. This ensures even baking times and a uniform appearance.

* Always preheat your oven so it is at the correct temperature when you put the cake in.

* Don't open the oven door to look at the cake during the first 10 or 15 minutes of baking. If you do, you will have a collapsed cake.

* If you think the cake may be browning too quickly, either turn the oven down a few degrees or slip a piece of foil over the cake to protect it.

* A cake should be cooked when it starts to shrink away from the sides of the tin.

* Always follow the cooling instructions because they vary depending on the type of cake.

* To remove cakes from a loose-bottomed cake tin, stand the base on a large tin so you can slip the sides down. The cake will be left on the tin base.

* Never fill or decorate a cake until it is completely cold.

* To enjoy cakes at their best, eat them as soon as you can. Otherwise, store in an airtight container in a cool place.

* Most of my cakes will freeze well as long as they are wrapped tightly in clingfilm or placed in a freezer bag. If the cake has been iced, open freezing is recommended, after which the cake needs to be sealed in a freezer bag. Remove from the bag before defrosting, otherwise the icing will stick.

* Leave cakes to defrost at room temperature for between three and four hours.

Equipment

You don't need all the latest equipment to make perfect cakes, but there are a few must haves:

* **Electric hand mixer** I rely heavily on my hand-held mixer because I like to feel the ingredients coming together, but if you prefer to use a free-standing food mixer, please do. Just remember to constantly scrape the mixture from down the sides of the bowl so it doesn't get left out of the mixing process.

* **Food processor** I use my processor only to make condensed milk, chop nuts and create purées because I find gluten- and wheat-free cakes just don't work if whizzed around in a processor. I'm sure there is a scientific reason for this, but I'm not quite sure what it is!

* **Whisks** I use a large balloon whisk quite a lot. They are great for getting air into a mixture without over beating.

* **Flexible silicone spatula** How did we ever cope without silicone? I use my spatula all the time when baking, especially for scraping down the sides of mixing bowls when creaming and beating and for making sure I get every scrap of mixture into the cake tin.

* **Scales** Baking is as much a science as an art, so scales are essential to achieving a perfect cake. I use battery-operated digital scales that can measure weights as well as volumes in metric and imperial. There are some really good inexpensive ones on the market now, so it's worth shopping around.

* **Measures** It really is worth purchasing a set of measuring spoons because the teaspoon in the kitchen drawer might not be the same size as mine!

* **Mixing bowls** I have lots of bowls in different sizes, but for a first time baker this isn't necessary. Invest in a couple of heatproof bowls of different sizes, making sure they have a rounded base so you can reach every bit of mixture.

* **Tins** Always buy the best you can afford. Cheap tins are a false economy because they don't perform well and don't last long. Good-quality tins that are looked after will last you a lifetime. Non-stick tins are a lot easier to clean, but it is still important to grease and line as recommended in each recipe. Always use the correct size tin for the recipe. If you don't have one, why not borrow one from a friend? I would recommend the following sizes, which will cover all the recipes in this book:

1 x 18cm (7 inch) square tin
with removable base

1 x 18cm (7 inch) deep round tin
with a removable base

2 x 20cm (8 inch) sandwich tins
with removable bases

1 x 20cm (8 inch) deep round tin
with a removable base

1 x 20cm (8 inch) springform sandwich tin

1 x 20cm (8 inch) square tin
with removable base

1 x 23cm (9 inch) springform sandwich tin
with a removable base

1 x 900g (2lb) loaf tin

1 x 33cm x 23cm (13 x 9 inch) Swiss roll tin

1 x 20cm x 30cm (8 x 12 inch) shallow
baking tin

1 x 25cm x 38cm (10 x 15 inch) Swiss roll
tin or roasting tin

1 x 18cm x 27cm (7 x 10½ inch) shallow
baking tin

6-hole muffin tin

12-hole muffin tin

* **Baking trays** These should always be heavy, flat and rigid.

* **Muffin cases** With the correct size paper cases, your cupcakes will rise beautifully and you shouldn't have any mixture left over. I use Easybake cases, the dimensions of which are 3.5cm (1¼ inches) high with a base width of 5cm (2 inches). You will, however, find a huge selection, in a variety of colours, in the supermarkets or at specialist cake decorating suppliers. Where cases are not required, you will need to grease and flour the muffin tins to stop the cakes sticking.

* **Wire/metal cooling rack** You need to cool cakes properly when they come out of the oven by letting the air circulate underneath.

* **Sieve** I always sift my dry ingredients as it helps to evenly combine xanthan gum, baking powder and spices into the flour. They are also good for straining purées and pulps and dusting cakes with icing sugar.

* **Knives** One of my best buys has been a large plastic knife normally used for cutting lettuce. It is brilliant for cutting brownies and other sticky cakes and traybakes. Palette and round-bladed knives are great for smoothing and lifting, whilst small serrated knives provide a clean finish.

* **Spoons** When folding flour, fruit or egg whites into the cake mixture, I always use a large metal serving spoon. It reduces the amount of folding I have to do and keeps more air in the mixture.

* **Skewers** I use a metal skewer to test whether my cakes are baked. Insert into the middle of the cake and if it comes out clean, the cake is ready.

* **Icing nozzles** I have a selection of different shapes and sizes for piping frosting onto my cupcakes. Unless you are an experienced cake decorator, you will need only a couple, in either plastic or metal.

* **Piping bag** Used for piping frostings and creams, they can be washable nylon or disposable plastic.

* **Baking parchment** Used for lining tins and trays. Don't make the mistake of using greaseproof paper. It is not stick-proof and you will need to grease it.

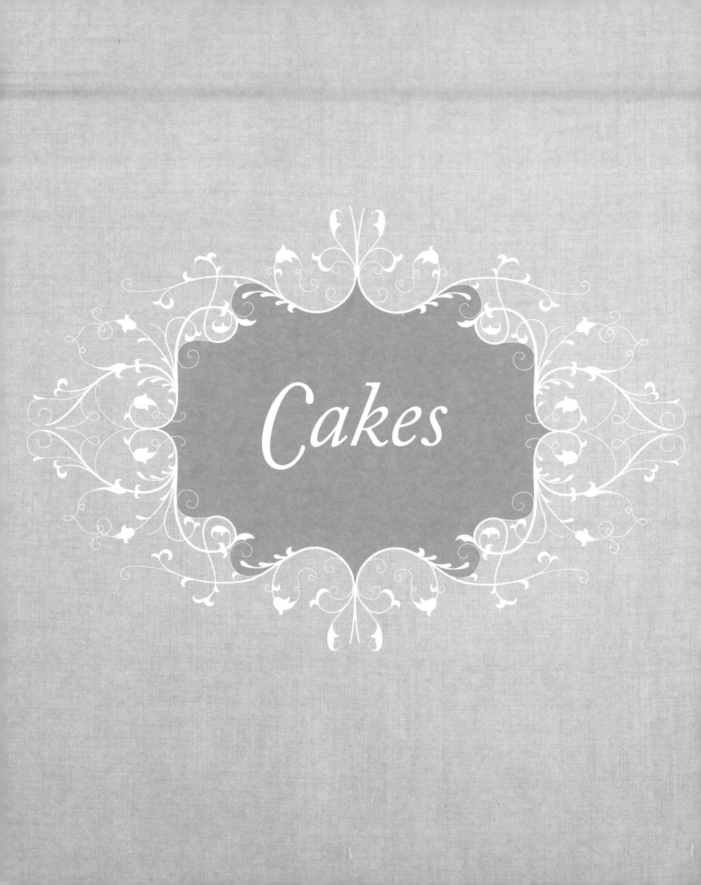

Cakes

Victoria sandwich

serves: 8 to 10
preparation: 25 minutes
baking: 20 minutes
cooling: 30 minutes
freeze: Yes, prior to filling

250g (9oz) eggs, beaten
   (about 4 large eggs)
1 tsp vanilla extract
2 tbsp soya/rice/almond milk
250g (9oz) dairy-free spread
250g (9oz) caster sugar
225g (8oz) wheat- and gluten-
   free self-raising flour
1 tsp xanthan gum
1½ tsp gluten-free
   baking powder
30g (1oz) ground almonds
Strawberry jam,
   for spreading
1 x Dairy-free Cream
   (see page 170)
2 tbsp caster sugar,
   for dusting

equipment
2 x 20cm (8 inch)
   sandwich tins

tip: If you don't need such
a large cake, halve the
ingredients and bake in two
15cm (6 inch) greased and
base-lined sandwich tins.
The baking time remains the
same – 20 minutes.

This is one of the most traditional and deliciously easy cakes you can bake, and for me it conjures up lazy Sunday afternoon teas and summer fêtes. It's an elegantly simple cake that I like to dress up with dairy-free cream and strawberry jam, but also tastes wonderful filled with dairy-free cream and passion fruit.

* Preheat the oven to 195°C/175°C fan/Gas 5. Grease the tins and line the bases with baking parchment.

* Blend the eggs, vanilla and milk together with a fork in a small bowl or jug. Using a hand-held electric mixer on a high setting, cream the dairy-free spread and sugar together in a large mixing bowl for about 3 minutes until light and fluffy.

* Gradually add the eggs, vanilla and milk mixture on a medium speed setting, mixing well between each addition. Don't worry if it curdles slightly, just turn the mixer setting to high for a couple of seconds and the mixture will become smooth again.

* Fold in the sifted flour, xanthan gum, baking powder and ground almonds using a large metal spoon so you don't knock the air out.

* Spoon the mixture into the two sandwich tins, smoothing to the edge with the back of a dessert spoon. To make sure both cakes are the same size, I weigh the two filled tins, adjusting if necessary.

* Bake for 20 minutes or until the cakes are well risen, golden and the sponges spring back when touched. You will also find that the sponges shrink from the sides of the tins once the cakes are cooked.

* Remove the baked cakes from the oven and cool in the tins for 10 minutes before turning them onto a metal cooling rack. Leave the paper bases on the cakes until completely cooled, as this will stop the sponges from shrinking.

* Once completely cool, place one cake on a cake board or serving plate and spread the jam evenly over the surface, then top with the dairy-free cream filling. Carefully place the other sponge on top and press down lightly to join the two. Dust with caster sugar and you are ready to serve.

Banana, pecan
& golden syrup loaf

serves: **8 to 10**
preparation: **20 minutes**
baking: **55 minutes**
cooling: **30 minutes**
freeze: **Yes**

100g (3½oz) dairy-free spread
50g (2oz) soft dark
   brown sugar
4 large eggs, beaten
225g (8oz) wheat- and gluten-
   free self-raising flour
1 tsp xanthan gum
4 ripe bananas, mashed
4 tbsp golden syrup
50g (2oz) pecan nuts,
   chopped

equipment
900g (2lb) loaf tin

'Yum,' my son Charlie said the first time he had a slice of this loaf, and I quite agree. For a very simple recipe, the addition of golden syrup makes this a wonderfully rich and flavoursome loaf with a soft and pillowy texture.

* Preheat the oven to 180°C/160°C fan/Gas 4. Grease and line the base and the sides of the loaf tin.

* In a large mixing bowl, use a hand-held electric mixer on a high speed setting to cream the dairy-free spread and sugar together for about 3 minutes until light and fluffy.

* Gradually add the beaten eggs on a medium speed setting. Don't worry if the mixture curdles slightly; you can turn the mixer setting up to high for a few seconds and the mixture will become smooth again.

* Sift the flour and xanthan gum into the mixture. Slowly fold in using a large metal spoon so you don't knock the air out. Slowly fold in the banana, golden syrup and the chopped pecan nuts until well combined.

* Spoon the mixture into the prepared tin, levelling the surface with the back of a dessert spoon.

* Bake for 50 to 55 minutes. Remove the cake from the oven, checking the loaf is cooked by inserting a metal skewer into the centre of the cake. If it comes out clean, the cake is baked. Cool in the tin for 10 minutes before turning out onto a metal cooling rack to completely cool.

tip: Don't be tempted to mix all the ingredients together at once, or the texture of the baked cake will be rubbery and dry.

Chocolate fudge cake

serves: **14**
preparation: **40 minutes**
baking: **1¼ to 1½ hours**
cooling: **Up to 1 hour**
freeze: **Yes, without the icing**

Death by chocolate, what a way to go! No chocolate cake is too rich for me and this one is certainly rich and gooey, just like a brownie, topped with a wonderfully dark and fudgy ganache. Don't worry if the top cracks and sinks a bit because, as with a good brownie, the top becomes crispy during baking and any defects are covered up with the fudge topping.

for the cake mixture

200g (7oz) good-quality (60% cocoa) dark dairy-free chocolate
200g (7oz) dairy-free spread
1 tbsp instant coffee granules mixed with 125ml (5fl oz) cold water
85g (3oz) wheat- and gluten-free plain flour
85g (3 oz) wheat- and gluten-free self-raising flour
1 tsp xanthan gum
¼ tsp bicarbonate of soda
200g (7oz) light muscovado sugar
200g (7oz) golden caster sugar
25g (1oz) cocoa powder
75ml (2½fl oz) soya/rice/almond milk
½ tbsp lemon juice
3 large eggs, beaten
100g (3½oz) bar white dairy-free chocolate, for decoration

ingredients continue...

* Preheat the oven to 160°C/140°C fan/Gas 3. Grease the tin and line the base with baking parchment.

* Melt the chocolate, dairy-free spread and coffee mixture over a medium heat in a heavy-based saucepan until everything has just melted. Or, if it's easier, in a suitable bowl in the microwave on high for about 1½ minutes. Remove from the microwave, stir and leave any unmelted bits of chocolate to finish melting.

* Whilst the chocolate is melting, in a big bowl mix the flours, xanthan gum, bicarbonate of soda, sugars and cocoa powder. Use your fingers to get rid of any lumps caused by the muscovado sugar.

* Heat your milk in the microwave on high for about 20 seconds or heat for a couple of minutes in a small heavy-based saucepan over a low heat. Take the milk off the heat, add the lemon juice and stir until the milk begins to thicken and look curdled. Congratulations, you now have dairy-free buttermilk.

* Beat the eggs in a separate bowl and add the dairy-free buttermilk.

* Add the melted chocolate mixture and the beaten egg/milk mixture into the flour mixture and, using a big metal spoon, stir until everything is well blended and you have a smooth, runny consistency.

* Pour the mixture into your prepared cake tin and bake in the oven for 1¼ to 1½ hours.

recipe continues...

for the fudge ganache

225g (8oz) good-quality (60% cocoa) dark dairy-free chocolate

55g (2oz) dark muscovado sugar

225g (8oz) dairy-free spread

5 tbsp dairy-free Evaporated Milk (see page 170)

½ tsp vanilla extract

equipment

20cm (8 inch) deep cake tin and swivel-bladed vegetable peeler

* Whilst the cake is baking, make the fudge ganache. Put the chocolate, muscovado sugar, dairy-free spread, dairy-free evaporated milk and vanilla extract into a heavy-based saucepan and heat gently, stirring constantly, until everything has melted. Pour into a bowl and leave to cool. Once cool, cover and place in the fridge for 1 hour or until spreadable.

* Once you think the cake is cooked, pierce the middle with a metal skewer and, if it comes out clean, then it is ready. Leave to cool in the tin for 30 minutes, then remove from the tin and cool completely on a metal cooling rack.

* When the cake has cooled, cut it in half horizontally, not worrying if the top cracks because this will be covered by the ganache. Sandwich the two halves together with a third of the ganache, then spread the remaining ganache over the top and sides of the cake, swirling it to give a frosted appearance.

* Holding the swivel-bladed vegetable peeler close to the edge of the bar of white dairy-free chocolate, run it along the top of the bar to shave off the curls. Sprinkle over the cake to decorate.

tip: Dab a small amount of apricot jam or glaze onto your cake board to hold the cake in place. It's a heavy cake and you don't want it to slip off.

Apple & blueberry cake

serves: **8 to 10**
preparation: **20 minutes**
baking: **2 hours**
cooling: **50 minutes**
freeze: **Yes**

325g (11½oz) wheat- and
   gluten-free self-raising flour
1 tsp xanthan gum
1 tsp ground mixed spice
Pinch of salt
225g (8oz) dairy-free spread
160g (5½oz) caster sugar
225g (8oz) blueberries
450g (1lb) cooking apples,
   peeled, cored and grated
3 large eggs, beaten
6 sugar cubes, crushed

equipment
2 x 20cm (8 inch)
   sandwich tins

I am always telling people that cake is good for you — it's the happy part of 'happy and healthy'. That might not be completely true, but this rustic tea-time treat is packed full of antioxidants and vitamin C and is totally delish.

* Preheat the oven to 180°C/160°C fan/Gas 4. Grease the cake tin and line the base and sides with baking parchment.

* Sift the flour, xanthan gum, mixed spice and salt into a large mixing bowl. Rub in the dairy-free spread until the mixture resembles fine breadcrumbs. Stir in the sugar, blueberries and apple. Add the beaten eggs and mix evenly.

* Spoon the mixture into the cake tin, smoothing the mixture evenly to the edge. Sprinkle the crushed sugar cubes evenly over the top of the mixture.

* Bake for 1½ to 2 hours or until a metal skewer inserted into the middle of the cake comes out clean. If the cake isn't ready, pop it back into the oven for a few more minutes.

* Remove the baked cake from the oven and leave to cool in the tin for 30 minutes, then turn out of the tin and finish cooling on a metal cooling rack.

tip: If you aren't that keen on blueberries or you haven't any to hand, substitute them with sultanas for an equally delicious tea-time treat.

Swirly blackcurrant cake

serves: 8 to 10
preparation: 30 minutes
baking: 35 to 40 minutes
cooling: 30 minutes
freeze: No

300ml (10fl oz) soya milk
1½ tbsp lemon juice
150g (5½oz) dairy-free spread
225g (8oz) caster sugar
3 large eggs, beaten
½ tsp vanilla extract
225g (8oz) wheat- and
  gluten-free plain flour
1 tsp xanthan gum
1½ tsp gluten-free
  baking powder
½ tsp bicarbonate of soda
115g (4 oz) blackcurrant
  conserve, plus 2 tbsp
  for the filling
1 x Dairy-free Cream
  (see page 170)
Icing sugar, for dusting

equipment
2 x 20cm (8 inch)
  sandwich tins

A really pretty cake that shrieks, 'Look at me'. It's full of fruity flavour and the blackcurrant conserve swirled through the sponge gives a traditional cake a beautiful twist.

* Preheat the oven to 170°C/150°C fan/Gas 3. Grease the tins and line the bases with baking parchment.

* Heat your soya milk in the microwave on high for 40 seconds or heat for a couple of minutes in a small heavy-based saucepan over a low heat. Take the milk off the heat, add the lemon juice and stir until the milk begins to thicken and look curdled, then put to one side. You now have dairy-free buttermilk.

* Using a hand-held electric mixer on a high speed setting, cream the dairy-free spread and sugar together for about 3 minutes until light and fluffy.

* Gradually add the beaten eggs and vanilla extract on a medium speed setting, mixing well between each addition. Don't worry if the mixture curdles slightly, just turn the mixer setting up to high for a couple of seconds and the mixture will become smooth again.

* Fold in half the sifted flour, the xanthan gum, baking powder and bicarbonate of soda until just combined, then fold in half the buttermilk until just combined. Fold in the remaining flour mixture, and then finally the remaining buttermilk.

* Spoon the mixture into two sandwich tins, smoothing to the edge with the back of a dessert spoon. To make sure both cakes are the same size, I weigh the two filled tins, adjusting if necessary.

* Stir the blackcurrant conserve in a small bowl until nice and smooth, then dot randomly over the two cake tins. Using a round-bladed knife, drag the jam in a swirling motion through the batter.

* Bake for 35 to 40 minutes or until the cakes start to shrink from the sides of the tins or a metal skewer inserted into the middle of the cakes comes out clean. If the cakes appear to be browning too quickly, cover with a piece of baking parchment or foil.

recipe continues...

* Remove the cakes from the oven, leaving them to cool in the tins for 10 minutes before turning out to cool on a metal cooling rack. Leave the paper bases on the cakes until completely cooled, as this will stop the sponges from shrinking.

* Once completely cool, place one cake on a cake board or serving plate, spread the dairy-free cream over the sponge and top with the remaining 2 tablespoons of blackcurrant conserve. Carefully place the other sponge on top and press down lightly to join the two. Dust the finished cake with icing sugar.

Bara brith

serves: **10**
preparation: **15 minutes +**
   overnight soaking
baking: **1½ to 1¾ hours**
cooling: **30 minutes**
freeze: **Yes**

450g (1lb) mixed dried
   fruits, currants,
   raisins, sultanas
250g (9oz) soft light
   brown sugar
300ml (10fl oz) warm
   black tea
2 tsp ground mixed spice
450g (1lb) wheat- and gluten-
   free self-raising flour
1 tsp xanthan gum
1 large egg, beaten

equipment
2 x 20cm (8 inch)
   sandwich tins

Being a good little Welsh girl, I had to include this version of the traditional tea loaf. Bara brith literally translates as 'speckled bread' and it is wonderful sliced and served warm with a good cuppa.

* In a large mixing bowl, soak the fruit and sugar overnight in the warm black tea.

* The next day, preheat the oven to 170°C/150°C fan/Gas 3. Grease and line the loaf tin.

* Mix the remaining ingredients into the fruit mixture and beat well to combine.

* Spoon the mixture into the lined loaf tin, levelling the surface with the back of your spoon. Bake for 1½ to 1¾ hours or until a metal skewer inserted into the middle of the cake comes out clean.

* Leave to cool in the tin for 10 minutes, then turn out onto a wire rack to finish cooling.

Date & chocolate torte

serves: **10 to 12**
preparation: **25 minutes**
baking: **35 minutes**
cooling: **30 minutes**
freeze: **No**

for the cake mixture
100g (3½oz) flaked almonds
125g (4½oz) good-quality (60% cocoa) dark dairy-free chocolate, chips or chopped
125g (4½oz) dried dates
3 large egg whites, at room temperature
125g (4½oz) caster sugar
30g (1oz) good-quality (60% cocoa) dark dairy-free chocolate, grated

for the coconut cream topping
250ml (9fl oz) coconut cream
1 tbsp icing sugar

equipment
20cm (8 inch) springform cake tin

A delicate, chewy and delicious torte that is really simple to make. I'm rather partial to it without the topping, but the coconut cream transforms it into a very glamorous pud.

* Preheat the oven to 180°C/160°C fan/Gas 4. Grease and line the base and sides of the cake tin.

* Put the almonds and chocolate in a food processor and process until fine. Finely chop the dates.

* Using a hand-held electric mixer on a high setting, whisk the egg whites in a large mixing bowl until they form soft peaks. Slowly add the sugar, whisking until the sugar dissolves.

* Fold in the almond and chocolate mixture, then the dates.

* Spoon the mixture into the tin, smoothing to the edge with the back of a dessert spoon.

* Bake for 30 to 35 minutes or until the mixture is set and starts to come away from the sides of the tin. Remove from the oven and leave to cool in the tin. Don't worry if the sides collapse in a bit, as this is quite normal for a torte made with egg whites. Once cool, turn out onto a serving plate.

* Using a free-standing food mixer, whisk the coconut cream for 10 minutes until soft peaks form, then add the icing sugar and whisk for a further minute.

* Spread the coconut cream over the top of the torte using a spatula or the back of a dessert spoon. Sprinkle with the grated chocolate to serve. Store in an airtight container for three days.

Orange
& pomegranate cake

serves: 8 to 10
preparation: 25 minutes
baking: 50 minutes
cooling: 1 hour 20 minutes
freeze: Yes

for the cake mixture
60g (2¼oz) crustless and
    stale wheat- and gluten-
    free white bread
200g (7oz) caster sugar
1½ tsp gluten-free
    baking powder
100g (3½ oz) ground
    almonds
200ml (7fl oz) sunflower oil
4 large eggs
½ tbsp Pomegranate
    Molasses (see page 169)
Zest of 1 large orange

for the pomegranate syrup
Juice of ½ large orange
½ tbsp Pomegranate
    Molasses (see page 169)
25g (1oz) caster sugar

equipment
20cm (8 inch) square tin

This is an amazingly delicious and moist cake, which can be either a tea-time treat or a spectacular dessert served with extra pomegranate syrup and dairy-free ice cream.

* Grease and line the base and the sides of the cake tin.

* Make breadcrumbs by placing the bread in a food processor and whizzing until you have quite a fine crumb. Combine the breadcrumbs with the caster sugar, baking powder and ground almonds in a big bowl.

* Whisk together the sunflower oil, eggs and pomegranate molasses in a separate bowl using a large balloon whisk. Stir this oil mixture into the dry ingredients, then add the grated orange zest and mix well.

* Pour the mixture into the prepared tin and put into a cold oven. Set the oven temperature to 180°C/160° fan/Gas 4 and bake for 45 minutes, then cover the cake with foil to cook for the last 5 minutes. Don't worry if it looks very dark, it should do.

* Whilst the cake is in the oven, make the syrup. Place the orange juice, pomegranate molasses and caster sugar into a small saucepan and heat gently for about 2 to 3 minutes until the sugar has dissolved and the liquid is syrupy. Don't worry if it isn't immediately thick and syrupy; as it cools, it will thicken up.

* Remove the cake from the oven and immediately make lots of holes over the top of the cake with a metal skewer. Gradually pour the syrup over the cake, using a pastry brush to spread it evenly.

* Leave the cake to stand for 1 hour, then carefully lift it out. Loosen the baking parchment before turning over onto another board, then remove the baking parchment. Turn it right side up onto a metal cooling rack and leave to cool. Cut into squares and serve with afternoon tea or as a wonderfully moreish dessert.

Traditional cherry
& almond cake

serves: 8
preparation: 25 minutes
baking: 1 hour
cooling: 35 minutes
freeze: Yes

250g (9oz) natural colour
   glacé cherries
100g (3½oz) ground almonds
185g (6½oz) wheat-
   and gluten-free
   self-raising flour
1 tsp xanthan gum
200g (7oz) dairy-free spread
200g (7oz) caster sugar
3 large eggs, beaten
Finely grated zest
   and juice of 1 lemon
6 white sugar cubes, crushed

equipment
20cm (8 inch) deep cake tin

tip: Always wash the syrup off glacé cherries before using in baking. This stops them from sinking to the bottom of the cake.

A truly traditional tea-time cake, this is wonderfully crunchy on top with a crispy edge and melt-in-the-mouth texture. My grandmother used to make this cake when she had guests for tea, and just the smell of it baking brings back memories of long summer holidays spent with my grandparents in Frinton-on-Sea.

* Preheat the oven to 180°C/160°C fan/Gas 4. Grease the cake tin, then line the base with baking parchment.

* Wash the sticky syrup off the cherries by rinsing them under the tap, then dry and chop into quarters. Mix the cherries with the ground almonds and 1 tablespoon of the flour.

* Sift the remaining flour and xanthan gum into a separate bowl.

* Using a hand-held electric mixer on a high setting, cream the dairy-free spread and sugar together for about 3 minutes until light and fluffy.

* Gradually add the beaten eggs on a medium speed setting, mixing well between each addition. Don't worry if the mixture curdles slightly; just turn the mixer setting up to high for a couple of seconds and the mixture will become smooth again.

* Fold in the sifted flour and xanthan gum using a large metal spoon so you don't knock the air out. Slowly fold in the cherry and ground almond mixture, again using the large metal spoon. Finally, fold in the grated lemon zest and juice.

* Spoon the mixture into the prepared tin and level out with the back of a dessert spoon. Make a small dip in the middle to stop the cake peaking during baking. Sprinkle the crushed sugar cubes evenly over the mixture.

* Bake for approximately 1 hour or until the cake is beginning to shrink away from the sides of the tin and is golden brown in colour. Remove from the oven and leave to cool in the tin for 15 minutes, then remove from the tin and cool completely on a metal cooling rack.

Raspberry, blueberry
& lime drizzle cake

makes: **16 squares**
preparation: **20 minutes**
baking: **55 minutes**
cooling: **30 minutes**
freeze: **Yes**

for the cake mixture
225g (8oz) dairy-free spread
225g (8oz) golden
caster sugar
4 large eggs, beaten
250g (9oz) wheat- and gluten-
free self-raising flour
1 tsp xanthan gum
Pinch of salt
25g (1oz) ground almonds
Grated zest and
juice of 2 limes
100g (3½oz) raspberries
100g (3½oz) blueberries

for the lime syrup
8 tbsp lime juice
(about 4 limes)
140g (5oz) caster sugar
Grated zest of 1 lime

equipment
20cm (8 inch) square tin

This cake is packed full of berries and has a lovely crunchy sugar topping. The limes cut through the sweetness beautifully and make a nice change to lemons.

* Preheat the oven to 180°C/160°C fan/Gas 4. Grease the cake tin and line the base and sides with baking parchment.

* In a large mixing bowl, use a hand-held electric mixer on a high speed setting to cream the dairy-free spread and caster sugar together.

* Gradually add the beaten eggs on a medium speed setting, mixing well between each addition. Don't worry if the mixture curdles slightly; just turn the mixer setting up to high for a couple of seconds and the mixture will become smooth again.

* Fold in the sifted flour, xanthan gum, salt, ground almonds and grated zest using a large metal spoon so you don't knock the air out. Add the berries and three tablespoons of the lime juice, folding them in carefully to create a lovely dropping consistency.

* Spoon the mixture into the cake tin, smoothing the mixture evenly to the edges.

* Bake for 55 minutes or until the cake is firm to the touch and golden brown in colour. If the cake appears to be browning too quickly, cover with a piece of baking parchment or silver foil.

* Whilst the cake is baking, you can make the syrup. Measure the lime juice and sugar into a bowl, add the lime zest and stir until blended.

* Remove the baked cake from the oven and whilst it is still hot, prick all over with a metal skewer and then slowly spoon the lime syrup all over. There will be a lot of syrup, but don't worry; if you spoon it slowly, the cake will absorb it all.

* When the cake is cold and the lime syrup absorbed, carefully turn out onto a metal cooling rack, removing the baking parchment.

tip: The photo shows you can add a variety of toppings to your cakes to make them fit for a party. Try dairy-free cream and fresh fruit.

Carrot cake

serves: **8 to 10**
preparation: **30 minutes**
baking: **1 hour 10 minutes**
cooling: **30 minutes**
freeze: **Yes**

for the cake mixture
100g (3½oz) walnuts, plus
  12 halves for decoration
2 large eggs (about 140g/5oz)
175g (6oz) soft dark
  brown sugar
Juice of ½ orange
Grated zest of 1 orange
150ml (5fl oz) sunflower oil
200g (7oz) wheat- and
  gluten-free plain flour
1 tsp xanthan gum
3 tsp ground mixed spice
1 tsp bicarbonate of soda
200g (7oz) coarsely
  grated carrots
115g (4oz) sultanas

for the orange syrup
Juice of ½ orange
1 tbsp lemon juice
75g (2¾oz) soft dark
  brown sugar

for the icing
175g (6oz) icing sugar
1½ to 2 tbsp orange juice

equipment
20cm (8 inch) deep round tin

This is a seriously sophisticated cake that doesn't rely on frosting for flavour. Rich, dark and full of flavour, it doesn't last long in our house and is a favourite with Cake Angels customers.

* Preheat the oven to 170°C/150°C fan/Gas 3. Grease the cake tin and line the base with baking parchment.

* Toast all the walnuts by spreading them out on a baking sheet and placing in the oven for 7 to 8 minutes. Once toasted, keep 12 halves for decorating the cake and finely chop the rest.

* Using a large balloon whisk, beat the eggs, sugar, orange juice, orange zest and oil together in a large mixing bowl.

* Fold in the sifted flour, xanthan gum, mixed spice and bicarbonate of soda with a large metal spoon to create a smooth batter. Fold in the grated carrots, sultanas and chopped walnuts.

* Spoon the mixture into the prepared tin and level with the back of a dessert spoon, creating a dip in the middle to prevent the cake from peaking during baking.

* Bake for 1 hour 10 minutes or until a metal skewer inserted into the middle of the cake comes out clean. Don't worry if the cake peaks and cracks a bit. It will settle quite a lot whilst cooling and will be covered by the icing.

* Whilst the cake is baking, heat the orange juice, lemon juice and soft dark brown sugar in a small heavy-based saucepan over a low heat. Don't let the syrup boil, but heat it enough to dissolve the sugar.

* Remove the baked cake from the oven and run a sharp knife round the edge. Pierce the cake all over with a metal skewer and slowly pour the orange syrup all over it, ensuring it soaks into the holes and round the edges. It takes a while for the cake to absorb all the syrup.

recipe continues...

* Leave the cake in the tin until it has cooled and all the syrup has been absorbed. Turn out, remove the baking parchment and leave to cool completely on a metal cooling rack.

* To make the icing, mix the sifted icing sugar with the orange juice until you have a nice thick spreading consistency. Pour over the cake, smoothing with a round-bladed knife or a palette knife and making sure to take the icing to the edge. Immediately decorate with the toasted walnut halves.

tip: This cake is so good it can be served without the icing, warmed and with a dollop of dairy-free cream or scoop of ice cream at a smart dinner party.

Chocolate
& hazelnut cake

serves: **8 to 10**
preparation: **25 minutes**
baking: **1 hour 10 minutes**
cooling: **50 minutes**
freeze: **No**

200g (7oz) hazelnuts
50g (2oz) good-quality
(60% cocoa) dark dairy-
free chocolate
1 tsp gluten-free
baking powder
100g (3½oz) dairy-free spread
5 large eggs, separated
175g (6oz) caster sugar
1 tsp vanilla extract
A pinch of salt

equipment
20cm (8 inch) springform
sandwich tin

This recipe was given to me by a good friend upon her return from a holiday in Italy, and I am very grateful. It is wonderfully light and nutty and goes down a treat with an espresso and the Sunday papers.

* Preheat the oven to 180°C/160°C fan/Gas 4. Grease and line the tin with baking parchment.

* Grind the hazelnuts, chocolate and baking powder together in a food processor until fine. Add the dairy-free spread to combine.

* Using a hand-held electric mixer on a high setting, cream the egg yolks and sugar together in a large mixing bowl until the mixture becomes thick and creamy. Add the hazelnut mixture and the vanilla extract and whisk until combined.

* In another bowl, use the hand-held electric mixer on a high speed setting to whisk the egg whites and salt together until stiff peaks form.

* Carefully fold the egg whites into the nut and chocolate mixture in three stages so you don't deflate the egg whites.

* Spoon the mixture into the prepared tin, smoothing to the edge with the back of a dessert spoon.

* Bake in the oven for 1 hour to 1 hour 10 minutes, or until the cake feels firm and a metal skewer inserted into the middle comes out clean.

* Remove from the oven and leave to cool in the tin for 15 minutes. Don't worry if the edges collapse a little, as this is quite normal for a cake made with whisked egg whites. Gently ease the sides of the cake out of the tin using a round-bladed knife, then leave on the base for another 15 minutes. Leave to cool completely on a metal cooling rack.

* Store in an airtight container for up to three days.

Orange, polenta & poppy seed cake

serves: **8 to 10**
preparation: **20 minutes**
baking: **55 minutes**
cooling: **35 minutes**
freeze: Yes

150g (5oz) coarse polenta
75g (3oz) wheat- and
    gluten-free plain flour
1 tsp xanthan gum
1½ tsp gluten-free baking
    powder
2 tsp poppy seeds
150g (5oz) caster sugar
2 large eggs, beaten plus
    2 egg whites
250g (9oz) soya yoghurt
125ml (4fl oz) sunflower oil
Grated zest and juice of
    1 medium orange

equipment
20cm (8 inch) deep round tin

An unpretentious cake that is light, moist and totally delicious. It keeps really well in an airtight tin ready for when friends drop in for an impromptu cup of coffee and a chat, or should I say gossip!

* Preheat the oven to 180°C/160°C fan/Gas 4. Grease the base and sides of the cake tin with parchment paper.
* Mix the polenta, flour, xanthan gum, baking powder and poppy seeds together in a mixing bowl.
* In another bowl with a hand-held electric mixer on a high speed setting whisk together the sugar, eggs and extra egg whites.
* Add the soya yoghurt, sunflower oil, zest and juice of the orange whisking until combined.
* Add the polenta mixture a little at a time, folding in with a large metal spoon between additions to make a nice thick batter.
* Spoon the mixture into the prepared tin, levelling the surface with the back of a desert spoon.
* Bake in the oven for 50 to 55 minutes or until the cake is firm to the touch and golden on top. A metal skewer inserted into the middle of the cake should come out clean.
* Remove the cake from the oven, leaving it to cool in the tin for 15 minutes, then remove from the tin and finish cooling on a metal cooling rack.

Christmas cake

serves: 8 to 10
preparation: 30 minutes
baking: 2½ hours
cooling: 1 hour 20 minutes
freeze: Yes, before icing

300g (10½oz) dairy-free
   spread
300ml (10fl oz) cranberry
   juice
300g (10½oz) runny honey
175g (6oz) dried sour
   cherries
175g (6oz) glacé cherries
350g (12oz) raisins
325g (11½oz) sultanas
1 tsp bicarbonate of soda
150g (5½oz) wheat- and
   gluten-free plain flour
1 tsp xanthan gum
150g (5½oz) ground almonds
½ tsp freshly grated nutmeg
100g (3½oz) candied mixed
   peel, finely diced
Brandy, for feeding
675g (1½lb) almond paste
   or marzipan
675g (1½lb) Dr. Oetker
   ready-to-roll icing

equipment
20cm (8 inch) deep round
   cake tin

My mother used to bake this cake every Christmas and I can vividly remember the kitchen being filled with the heady smell of baking fruit and spices. It is the best fruit cake I have ever tasted, and my customers must agree because I sell out every year!

* Preheat the oven to 160°C/140°C fan/Gas 3. Grease the cake tin and line the base and sides with baking parchment.

* Melt the dairy-free spread, cranberry juice and honey in a large heavy-based saucepan.

* Stir in the sour cherries, glacé cherries, raisins and sultanas, bring to the boil and reduce to a simmer over a low heat for 5 minutes, when the fruit should be plump and luscious.

* Transfer the mixture to a large mixing bowl and stir in the bicarbonate of soda. The mixture will fizz furiously for a while. Leave to cool for 10 minutes.

* Fold the flour, xanthan gum, ground almonds, nutmeg and candied peel with a large metal spoon into the fruit mixture. Spoon the mixture into the prepared cake tin and level with the back of a dessert spoon.

* Tear off a piece of baking parchment large enough to cover the top of the tin and halfway down the side of the tin. Cut a small circle out of the middle of the paper. Lay the paper over the top of the tin and tie it in place with string. Wrap a sheet of brown paper round the tin again, tying in place with string. This is to protect the cake during the long baking time. Place on a baking tray because a small amount of grease will seep out the bottom of the tin.

* Bake in the preheated oven for 2½ hours or until a metal skewer inserted into the middle of the cake comes out clean. Leave in the tin to cool for 1 hour.

* Run a knife round the collar of the cake, remove the cake from the tin and leave to finish cooling on a metal cooling rack.

* When completely cool, pierce the surface of the cake with a metal skewer and feed with a couple of tablespoons of brandy.

recipe continues...

tip: You can make this cake up to a month in advance, storing in a cool place and feeding regularly until you are ready to cover it in almond paste and icing. If you don't like almond paste or icing, this cake tastes just as good with a light dusting of icing sugar.

* Wrap the completely cold cake in a double layer of baking parchment and again in foil and store in a cool place, feeding at intervals with brandy. (I like to feed my Christmas cakes with 2 tablespoons of brandy every other day for two weeks before icing.)

* A week before Christmas, cover the whole cake or just the top of the cake with almond paste or marzipan.

* Leave at least a day before covering with ready-to-roll icing and decorating.

Chocolate banana loaf

serves: 8
preparation: 15 minutes
baking: 55 minutes
cooling: 25 minutes
freeze: Yes

3 ripe bananas, mashed
170g (6oz) caster sugar
185g (6½oz) wheat-
    and gluten-free
    self-raising flour
1 tsp xanthan gum
2 large eggs, beaten
3 tbsp sunflower oil
3 tbsp soya/rice/
    almond milk
100g (3½oz) good-quality
    (60% cocoa) dark dairy-
    free chocolate, grated
90g (3oz) walnuts, chopped

equipment
900g (2lb) loaf tin

At some time or other, we all have bananas that need to be used up, and banana bread is an ideal way of doing this. If, however, you really want to treat yourself, try adding chocolate. It transforms the loaf into a rich and moist indulgence.

* Preheat the oven to 180°C/160°C fan/Gas 4. Grease and line the loaf tin.

* Mix the mashed bananas and sugar in a large bowl until just combined. Add the sifted flour, xanthan gum, eggs, oil and milk and stir gently with a large metal spoon until just combined. Add the grated chocolate and chopped walnuts.

* Spoon the mixture into the prepared loaf tin, levelling with the back of a dessert spoon.

* Bake for 55 minutes or until a metal skewer inserted into the middle of the cake comes out clean. Remove from the oven and cool in the tin for 5 minutes, then turn out onto a metal cooling rack.

Apricot & squash torte

serves: **12**
preparation: **45 minutes**
baking: **45 minutes**
cooling: **1 hour**
freeze: **Yes**

300g (10½oz) butternut
  squash, peeled
  and deseeded
1 tsp bicarbonate of soda
175g (6oz) caster sugar
3 tbsp runny honey
150g (5½oz) dairy-free spread
Grated zest of 1 orange
3 large eggs, beaten
½ tsp vanilla extract
150g (5½oz) wheat- and
  gluten-free plain flour
1 tsp xanthan gum
50g (2oz) ground almonds
1½ tsp gluten-free
  baking powder
115g (4oz) dried apricots,
  finely chopped
15g (½oz) flaked almonds
Icing sugar, for dusting

equipment
23cm (9 inch) springform
  sandwich tin

I have served this torte as a dessert at quite a few dinner parties and nobody has ever guessed that it contains a vegetable! The colour has always been much admired and I know everyone has enjoyed it because there is never any left, much to my husband's disappointment.

* Preheat the oven to 180°C/160°C fan/Gas 4. Grease and line the base of the tin.

* Cut the prepared squash into small chunks and place in a small heavy-based saucepan covered with water. Bring to the boil and simmer for 25 to 30 minutes or until the squash is very soft. Take off the heat, drain and purée in a food processor.

* Stir the bicarbonate of soda into the squash purée and set aside to cool.

* In a large mixing bowl, use a hand-held electric mixer on a high setting to cream the sugar, honey, dairy-free spread and orange zest together.

* Gradually add the eggs and vanilla extract on a medium speed setting, mixing well between each addition. Don't worry if it curdles slightly; just turn the mixer setting to high for a couple of seconds and the mixture will become smooth again.

* Sift the flour, xanthan gum, ground almonds and baking powder into the mixture. Add the puréed squash and apricots and fold everything in carefully. The mixture will curdle, but don't worry.

* Spoon the mixture into the prepared tin, smoothing to the edge with the back of a dessert spoon. Sprinkle the flaked almonds evenly over the top of the torte.

* Bake in the oven for 35 to 45 minutes until the torte shrinks away slightly from the sides of the tin. If you need to bake it for 45 minutes, place a foil cover over the cake for the last 10 minutes.

* Remove the baked torte from the oven and cool in the tin for 10 minutes before turning it out onto a metal cooling rack.

* Dust with icing sugar. The cake can be stored in an airtight container for up to three days.

Greek honey
& pine nut cake

serves: **8 to 10**
preparation: **25 minutes**
baking: **50 minutes**
cooling: **30 minutes**
freeze: **Yes**

for the cake mixture
50g (2oz) pine nuts, plus
    1 tablespoon for topping
115g (4oz) dairy-free spread
80g (3oz) caster sugar
80g (3oz) runny honey
Grated zest of 1 orange
2 large eggs, beaten
175g (6oz) wheat- and
    gluten-free plain flour
1 tsp gluten-free baking
    powder
¼ tsp bicarbonate of soda
1 tsp cinnamon
1 tsp xanthan gum
75ml (2½fl oz) soya/rice/
    almond milk
50g (2oz) coarse polenta

for the orange syrup
2 tbsp runny honey
Juice of 1 orange

equipment
20cm (8 inch) deep round tin

When our neighbour returned from her holiday in Greece, she bought us a wonderful jar of Greek honey as a gift for watering her plants. This gave me just the excuse I needed to bake this moist and crunchy cake, so reminiscent of the honey-drenched cakes eaten whilst on summer holidays in the Greek Islands.

* Preheat the oven to 170°C/150°C fan/Gas 3. Grease and line the base and the sides of the cake tin.

* Toast 50g (2oz) of the pine nuts on a baking tray in the oven for approximately 5 to 6 minutes. Keep an eye on them because they can go from nicely browned to burnt very quickly. Remove from the oven and leave to cool.

* In a large mixing bowl, use a hand-held electric mixer on a high setting to cream the dairy-free spread, sugar, honey and orange zest together for about 3 minutes until light and fluffy.

* Gradually add the beaten eggs on a medium setting. Don't worry if the mixture curdles slightly; you can turn the mixer setting up to high for a few seconds and the mixture will become smooth again.

* Sift the flour, baking powder, bicarbonate of soda, cinammon and xanthan gum into the mixture. Slowly fold in with the pine nuts using a large metal spoon so you don't knock the air out.

* Slowly fold in half the milk, then fold in half the polenta, the remaining half of milk and then the remaining half of the polenta.

* Spoon the mixture into the prepared tin, levelling the surface with the back of a dessert spoon and making a small dip in the middle to stop the cake peaking whilst baking. Scatter the remaining tablespoon of untoasted pine nuts over the surface of the mixture.

* Bake for 45 to 50 minutes until slightly risen, golden and firm to the touch.

recipe continues...

* Whilst the cake is baking, make the syrup by mixing the runny honey and orange juice together in a small heavy-based saucepan. Bring slowly to the boil and simmer for 5 minutes without stirring. The syrup will not be thick and sticky, but it will coat the back of a wooden spoon. Leave to cool slightly.

* Remove the cake from the oven, leaving it to cool in the tin for 10 minutes. Turn out onto a metal cooling rack over a large serving plate.

* Whilst the cake is still warm, prick it all over with a metal skewer, being careful not to pierce the bottom of the cake, and carefully pour over the syrup. Be patient and let the syrup slowly soak into the cake. Any that dribbles off will collect on the plate and can be used again.

tip: If you can, use a dark runny Greek honey. If not, an English runny honey will be fine; it just won't have that distinctive Greek taste and aroma.

Boiled fruit cake

serves: **8 to 10**
preparation: **30 minutes**
baking: **2 hours**
cooling: **40 minutes**
freeze: **Yes**

400g (14oz) Dairy-free
  Condensed Milk
  (see page 167)
150g (5½oz) dairy-free spread
225g (8oz) raisins
225g (8oz) sultanas
175g (6oz) currants
175g (6oz) glacé cherries,
  chopped
225g (8oz) wheat- and gluten-
  free self-raising flour
1 tsp xanthan gum
2 tsp ground mixed spice
1 tsp ground cinnamon
2 large eggs

equipment
18cm (7 inch) deep round tin

I had been curious about this fruit cake for a long time, but because it contained condensed milk, I thought I would never get to try it. Then I discovered how to make dairy-free condensed milk and I'm so glad I did. I love this cake – it is so easy to make and yet tastes just like Granny used to make – and it keeps for ages.

* Preheat the oven to 150°C/130°C fan/Gas 2. Grease and line the base and sides of the cake tin with baking parchment.

* Place the dairy-free condensed milk into a large heavy-based saucepan and add the dairy-free spread, dried fruit and glacé cherries. Heat over a low heat until the dairy-free spread has melted, then stir and simmer gently for 5 minutes. Remove from the heat and put to one side to cool for 10 minutes.

* Sift the flour, xanthan gum and spices into a large mixing bowl and make a well in the centre.

* Add the eggs and the cooled fruit. Mix together quickly until combined. Spoon the mixture into the prepared cake tin.

* Bake in the oven for 1¾ to 2 hours or until the cake has risen, is firm to the touch and golden brown and a metal skewer inserted into the middle of the cake comes out clean.

* Remove from the oven and leave to cool in the tin for 10 minutes. Remove from the tin, peel off the baking parchment and continue to cool on a metal cooling rack.

* Store wrapped in baking parchment in an airtight tin. If stored properly, fruit cake can last at least a month!

Marmalade, hazelnut & chocolate torte

serves: **10 to 12**
preparation: **30 minutes**
baking: **1 hour**
cooling: **40 minutes**
freeze: Yes

175g (6oz) dairy-free spread
175g (6oz) good-quality
   (60% cocoa) dark dairy-
   free chocolate
5 large eggs, separated
175g (6oz) caster sugar
150g (5½oz) hazelnuts,
   ground in a food
   processor with skins on
200g (7oz) fine-cut
   marmalade
Finely grated zest
   of 1 orange
1 tsp cocoa powder,
   for dusting

equipment
23cm (9 inch) springform
   sandwich tin

If, like me, you love chocolate oranges, then this really is the cake for you. Rich and intense in flavour, this cake needs only a light dusting of cocoa powder to set it off to perfection.

* Preheat the oven to 190°C/170°C fan/Gas 5. Grease and line the base of the cake tin.

* Melt the dairy-free spread and dairy-free chocolate together in a heatproof bowl over a simmering saucepan of water. Don't let the bottom of the bowl touch the water.

* Whisk the eggs yolks and sugar together in a separate bowl, using a hand-held electric mixer on a high speed setting, until the mixture is thick and creamy.

* Take the melted chocolate mixture off the heat and mix in the ground hazelnuts, marmalade and orange zest.

* In a large, spotlessly clean bowl, whisk the egg whites until stiff peaks form.

* Fold the egg yolk and sugar mixture into the chocolate and mix until it is all combined. Gently fold in the egg whites in three stages so you don't knock out the air.

* Spoon the mixture into the prepared tin, levelling the surface with the back of a dessert spoon.

* Bake in the oven for 20 minutes, then reduce the oven temperature to 170°C/150°C fan/Gas 3 for a further 35 to 40 minutes. Check the cake is baked by inserting a metal skewer into the centre of the cake, if it comes out clean, then the cake is ready.

* Remove the cake from the oven, leaving it to cool in the tin for 20 minutes, then remove from the tin and cool completely on a metal cooling rack. Finally, dust with cocoa powder before serving.

Coffee & walnut cake

serves: **8 to 10**
preparation: **45 minutes**
baking: **30 minutes**
cooling: **30 minutes**
freeze: **No**

for the cake mixture
75g (2¾oz) walnut halves
175g (6oz) dairy-free spread
175g (6oz) soft light
   brown sugar
3 large eggs, beaten
175g (6oz) wheat- and gluten-
   free self-raising flour
1 tsp xanthan gum
1½ tsp gluten-free
   baking powder
1½ tbsp instant coffee,
   mixed with 2 tbsp
   boiling water

for the coffee cream filling
1 x Dairy-free Cream
   (see page 170)
2 tsp espresso or strong
   filter coffee

for the coffee syrup
1 heaped tbsp instant coffee
50g (2oz) demerara sugar

for the coffee icing
200g (7oz) icing sugar
2 tbsp espresso or strong
   filter coffee

equipment
2 x 20cm (8inch)
   sandwich tins

I'm not a great coffee drinker, but I just adore this Coffee and Walnut Cake, probably because the syrup makes it so wonderfully moist and the coffee icing is chewy and luscious.

* Preheat the oven to 170°C/150°C fan/Gas 3. Grease the two sandwich tins and then line the bases with baking parchment.

* Toast all your walnuts by spreading them out on a baking sheet and placing in the oven for 7 to 8 minutes. Once toasted, keep 12 halves for decorating the cake and finely chop the rest.

* In another bowl and using a hand-held electric mixer on a high setting, cream the dairy-free spread and soft light brown sugar together for about 3 minutes until light and fluffy.

* Gradually add the beaten eggs on a medium speed setting, mixing well between each addition. Don't worry if the mixture curdles slightly; just turn the mixer setting up to high for a couple of seconds and the mixture will become smooth again.

* Sift the flour, xanthan gum and baking powder and fold into the eggs using a large metal spoon so you don't knock the air out. Add the coffee and walnut pieces, carefully folding in until the mixture is nice and smooth.

* Spoon the mixture into the two sandwich tins, smoothing to the edge with the back of a dessert spoon. To make sure both cakes are the same size, I weigh the two filled tins, adjusting if necessary.

* Bake for 30 minutes or until the cakes begin to shrink away from the side of the tins.

* Whilst the cakes are baking, you can make up the syrup. Place the coffee and sugar into a heatproof jug and then measure 55ml (2fl oz) boiling water into it, stirring briskly until the coffee and sugar have dissolved. This should take about a minute.

* Remove the baked cakes from the oven, leaving them in their tins. Whilst they are still hot, prick them all over with a metal skewer. Spoon the syrup all over as evenly as possible. Leave in the tins to soak up all the syrup.

recipe continues...

* When the cakes are cold, carefully turn them out, removing the baking parchment. Place one cake upside down on a cake board or serving plate.

* Mix the coffee into the dairy-free cream and spread all over the base cake. Carefully place the other cake on top.

* Make the coffee icing by sifting the icing sugar into a bowl and then blending in the coffee. If the icing is a bit runny, just add a little more icing sugar. You need the icing to be a smooth consistency and not too runny. Using a round-bladed knife or palette knife, smooth the icing over the cake. Decorate with the 12 roasted walnut halves.

tip: You can make the coffee syrup, filling and icing stronger if you are a real coffee addict.

Raspberry
& almond cake

serves: 8 to 10
preparation: 30 minutes
baking: 1¼ hours
cooling: 15 to 35 minutes
freeze: Yes

for the cake mixture
175g (6oz) dairy-free spread
175g (6oz) caster sugar
½ tsp vanilla extract
3 large eggs, beaten
80g (3oz) wheat- and gluten-
  free self-raising flour
1 tsp xanthan gum
½ tsp gluten-free baking
  powder
115g (4oz) ground almonds
175g (6oz) fresh or frozen
  raspberries

for the almond topping
15g (½oz) dairy-free spread
50g (2oz) flaked almonds
15g (½oz) caster sugar
Icing sugar, for dusting

equipment
20cm (8 inch) deep round tin

This cake smells absolutely delicious whilst baking, with the aroma of toasting almonds and a hint of sweet raspberries – yum.

* Preheat the oven to 180°C/160°C fan/Gas 4. Grease and line the base and sides of the cake tin.

* In a large mixing bowl, use a hand-held electric mixer on a high speed setting to cream the dairy-free spread, sugar and vanilla extract for about 3 minutes until light and fluffy.

* Gradually add the beaten eggs on a medium speed setting. Don't worry if the mixture curdles slightly; you can turn the mixer setting up to high for a few seconds and the mixture will become smooth again.

* Sift the flour, xanthan gum, baking powder and ground almonds into the mixture. Fold in slowly using a large metal spoon so you don't knock the air out.

* Gently fold in the raspberries, being careful not to break them up.

* Spoon the mixture into the prepared tin and level out with the back of a dessert spoon.

* Make the topping by melting the dairy-free spread in a small heavy-based saucepan over a gentle heat. Once melted, remove from the heat. Stir in the flaked almonds and caster sugar.

* Sprinkle the mixture over the top of the cake, making sure you go right to the edge.

* Bake for 1 hour to 1¼ hours or until the cake begins to shrink away from the sides of the tin and a metal skewer pierced into the middle of the cake comes out clean.

* Remove the cake from the oven, leaving it to cool in the tin for 15 minutes, then remove from the tin and dust with icing sugar. Either cool completely on a metal cooling rack or serve warm with dairy-free ice cream for a delicious pud.

Chocolate orange
drizzle cake

serves: 8
preparation: 25 minutes
baking: 50 minutes
cooling: 30 minutes
freeze: Yes

This was my mother's favourite cake and for years I have tried to replicate the lovely crunchy sugar coating hiding underneath the chocolate top. I have found the best way to achieve this is to use granulated sugar with the orange juice and to drizzle it over a still-warm cake – perfect.

for the cake mixture
3 large eggs, beaten
6 tbsp soya/rice/almond milk
140g (5oz) dairy-free spread
225g (8oz) caster sugar
Finely grated zest of
   1 large orange
175g (6oz) wheat- and
   gluten-free flour
1 tsp xanthan gum
1½ tsp gluten-free
   baking powder
50g (2oz) ground almonds

for the orange syrup
3 tbsp orange juice,
   fresh is nicest
50g (2oz) granulated sugar

for the chocolate icing
100g (3½oz) dairy-free
   milk chocolate
30ml (1fl oz) sunflower oil

equipment
900g (2lb) loaf tin

* Preheat the oven to 180°C/160°C fan/Gas 4. Grease the loaf tin.

* Beat the eggs and milk together in a small bowl and put to one side.

* In a large mixing bowl, use a hand-held electric mixer on a high speed setting to cream together the dairy-free spread, sugar and orange zest for about 3 minutes until light and fluffy.

* Gradually add the beaten eggs and milk on a medium speed setting, mixing well between each addition. Don't worry if the mixture curdles slightly; just turn the mixer setting up to high for a few seconds and the mixture will become smooth again.

* Carefully fold in the sifted flour, xanthan gum, baking powder and ground almonds using a large metal spoon so you don't knock the air out. Spoon the mixture into the prepared tin, levelling with the back of a dessert spoon.

* Bake in the oven for 45 to 50 minutes until the sponge has risen and is firm to the touch.

* Whilst the cake is baking, make the syrup. In a small bowl, mix together the orange juice and granulated sugar, stirring until the sugar begins to dissolve. Put to one side.

* Remove the cake from the oven and, as soon as possible, remove from the tin and peel off the baking parchment. Place on a metal cooling rack. Using a metal skewer, immediately pierce holes all over the top of the cake, being carefully not to pierce all the way through.

* Whilst the cake is still warm, gradually spoon the syrup all over, letting it soak slowly into the cake. Leave to cool completely.

recipe continues...

* Bring water to the boil in a small heavy-based saucepan, remove from the heat and place a heatproof bowl over it containing the milk chocolate and sunflower oil. Keep stirring until it is melted and combined.

* Pour the melted chocolate over the cake, letting it dribble slightly down the sides. You need only a thin layer of chocolate: if it is too thick, you won't be able to cut the cake. Once the chocolate has set, use a sharp knife to slice the cake.

Light chocolate torte

serves: 8 to 10
preparation: 20 minutes
baking: 40 minutes
cooling: 35 minutes
freeze: Yes

200g (7oz) good-quality (60% cocoa) dark dairy-free chocolate
1 tbsp brandy
1 tbsp strong black coffee
150g (5½oz) caster sugar
150g (5½oz) dairy-free spread
100g (3½oz) ground almonds
5 medium eggs, separated
Cocoa powder, for dusting

equipment
20cm (8 inch) deep round tin

When you are in the mood for something sweet and chocolaty, but not too rich, then this is the cake for you. It is wonderfully light and gooey and makes a perfect dinner party or supper dessert served with ice cream and berries.

* Preheat the oven to 180°C/160°C fan/Gas 4. Grease the cake tin and line the base and sides with baking parchment.

* Place the chocolate, brandy, coffee, sugar and dairy-free spread into a heatproof bowl and place over a pan of simmering water. Make sure the bottom of the bowl doesn't touch the water. Stir well and once melted, remove from the heat and leave to cool.

* Stir in the ground almonds, then the egg yolks, one by one, until all are combined.

* In a separate clean and dry bowl, use a hand-held electric mixer on a high speed to whisk the egg whites until they form soft peaks. Carefully fold the whisked egg whites into the chocolate mixture until combined.

* Spoon the mixture into the prepared tin, levelling the surface with the back of a dessert spoon.

* Bake in the oven for 35 to 40 minutes, depending on how squidgy you like your torte to be.

* Remove the baked cake from the oven, leaving it to cool in the tin for 15 minutes, then remove from the tin and finish cooling on a metal cooling rack. Dust with cocoa powder.

Red velvet cake

serves: 14 to 16
preparation: 30 minutes
baking: 30 minutes
cooling: 45 minutes
freeze: No

The most amazing cake you will ever bake – a real showstopper that loves nothing more than being the centre of attention (see picture on page 60). The chocolate and hazelnut filling is totally delicious on its own, but sandwiched between layers of rich, red sponge, it has been known to bring seasoned cake-eaters to their knees. Best of all, it's a really easy cake to make.

for the cake mixture
120g (4½oz) hazelnuts
240ml (8fl oz) soya milk
1½ tbsp lemon juice
120g (4½oz) dairy-free spread
300g (10½oz) caster sugar
2 large eggs, beaten
20g (¾oz) cocoa powder
40ml (½fl oz) red food
    colouring (Silver Spoon
    or Dr. Oetker)
1 tsp vanilla extract
3 tsp white wine vinegar
300g (10½oz) wheat-
    and gluten-free
    self-raising flour
2 tsp xanthan gum
1 tsp salt
1 tsp bicarbonate of soda

ingredients continue...

* Preheat the oven to 170°C/150°C fan/Gas 3. Grease the tins and then line the bases with baking parchment.

* Toast all the hazelnuts by spreading them out on a baking sheet and placing in the oven for 7 to 8 minutes. Once toasted, chop and put to one side.

* Heat the soya milk in a small saucepan over a gentle heat until warm or heat in a microwave on high for 40 seconds. Take the milk off the heat, add the lemon juice and stir until the milk begins to thicken and look curdled, then put to one side. You now have dairy-free buttermilk.

* Using a hand-held electric mixer on a high setting, cream the dairy-free spread and sugar together for about 5 minutes in a large mixing bowl until light and fluffy.

* Gradually add the eggs on a medium speed setting, mixing well between each addition. Don't worry if it curdles slightly; just turn the mixer setting to high for a couple of seconds and the mixture will become smooth again.

* In a separate bowl, mix together the cocoa powder, red food colouring, vanilla extract and white wine vinegar to make a thick, dark paste. Add to the egg mixture and mix thoroughly until combined.

* Sift the flour, xanthan gum, salt and bicarbonate of soda together into a small bowl.

* Using a large metal spoon, fold half the soya milk into the mixture, followed by half the flour, then repeat the process until all the milk and flour have been incorporated.

recipe continues...

for the chocolate and hazelnut filling

115g (4oz) coconut oil
45g (1½oz) cocoa powder
85ml (3fl oz) runny honey
225g (8oz) good-quality
    (60% cocoa) dark
    dairy-free chocolate,
    chips or chopped
3 tbsp hazelnut oil
Pinch of salt
2 tsp vanilla extract
175g (6oz) hazelnut butter
    (or 175g/6oz skinned
    and roasted hazelnuts
    whizzed into a paste
    in a food processor)

for the frosting

170g (6oz) icing sugar
¼ tsp cream of tartar
1 medium egg white
Small pinch of salt

equipment

3 x 20cm (8 inch)
    sandwich tins

* Spoon the mixture into the three sandwich tins, smoothing to the edge with the back of a dessert spoon.

* Bake in the oven for 25 to 30 minutes or until the cakes are risen and firm to the touch.

* Whilst the cakes are baking, make the chocolate and hazelnut filling. Place the coconut oil, cocoa powder and honey in a small heavy-based saucepan over a gentle heat and mix until combined, then add the chocolate and stir until melted.

* Add the hazelnut oil, salt, vanilla extract and hazelnut butter and stir until smooth. Don't allow the mixture to boil; it just needs to be warm enough to melt the chocolate. Pour into a jar and cool in the fridge until needed.

* Remove the baked cakes from the oven and cool in the tins for 10 minutes before turning them onto a metal cooling rack. Leave the paper bases on the cakes until completely cooled (this will stop the sponges from shrinking).

* Whilst the cakes are cooling, make the frosting. Measure all the ingredients and 2 tbsp water into a heatproof bowl over a saucepan of boiling water. Stir with a metal spoon to dissolve the sugar – this takes exactly 2 minutes.

* Remove the bowl from the heat and, with a hand-held electric mixer on a high speed setting, whisk for 9 minutes. The frosting will now be cool and stand up in soft peaks.

* Place one cake on a cake board or serving plate and spread with the chocolate and hazelnut filling, then carefully place the second sponge on top and press down lightly to join the two. Spread the top of this cake with more chocolate and hazelnut filling, then carefully place the third cake on top, pressing down lightly to join the other two.

* Working quickly as the frosting sets rapidly, cover the top and sides of the cake, swirling the icing to form soft peaks. Pat the toasted and chopped hazelnuts round the sides of the cake.

* Leave the cake to set in a cool place, but not the fridge, before serving. Store in an airtight container for up to two days.

tip: If you have any chocolate and hazelnut filling left over, store it in a covered container in the fridge and use it to spread on pancakes or on top of ice cream.

Lemon curd sponge

serves: **8 to 10**
preparation: **25 minutes**
baking: **40 minutes**
cooling: **30 minutes**
freeze: **No**

This was one of the first cakes I baked after removing dairy products from my diet. It took me a while to perfect the lemon curd, but it was well worth the effort and it is still one of my favourite cakes.

for the cake mixture
225g (8oz) dairy-free spread
225g (8oz) golden
    granulated sugar
Finely grated zest and
    juice of 1 lemon
4 large eggs, beaten
50ml (2fl oz) soya
    double cream
225g (8oz) wheat- and gluten-
    free self-raising flour
1 tsp xanthan gum
2 tsp gluten-free
    baking powder

for the lemon syrup
Juice of 2 lemons
100g (3½oz) golden
    granulated sugar

for the filling
1 x Lemon Curd
    (see page 168)
1 x Dairy-free Cream
    (see page 170)

equipment
2 x 20cm (8 inch)
    sandwich tins

* Preheat the oven to 190°C/170°C fan/Gas 5. Grease the two tins and line the bases with baking parchment.

* Using a hand-held electric mixer on a high setting, cream the dairy-free spread, sugar and lemon zest together in a large mixing bowl for about 3 minutes until light and fluffy.

* Gradually add the eggs, soya cream and lemon juice on a medium speed setting, mixing well between each addition. Don't worry if it curdles slightly; just turn the mixer setting to high for a couple of seconds and the mixture will become smooth again.

* Fold in the sifted flour, xanthan gum and baking powder using a large metal spoon so you don't knock the air out.

* Spoon the mixture into the two sandwich tins, smoothing to the edge with the back of a dessert spoon. To make sure both cakes are the same size, I weigh the two filled tins, adjusting if necessary.

* Bake for 35 to 40 minutes or until the cakes are well risen, golden and the sponges spring back when touched. You will also find the sponges shrink from the sides of the tin once the cakes are cooked.

* Whilst the cakes are baking, make the lemon syrup by combining the sugar and lemon juice in a small bowl and stirring well to combine.

* Remove the baked cakes from the oven and gradually spoon the lemon syrup over both. Leave the cakes to cool in the tins for 10 minutes before turning them out onto a metal cooling rack.

* Once completely cool, place one cake on a cake board or serving plate and spread the lemon curd evenly over the surface, then top with the dairy-free cream filling.

* Carefully place the other sponge on top and press down lightly to join the two.

* Store in an airtight container for up to three days.

tip: Try this with Passion Fruit Butter (see page 169).

Le Fraisier

serves: 8 to 10
preparation: 1½ hours
baking: 40 minutes
cooling: up to 4 hours
freeze: Yes

for the cake mixture
4 large eggs, separated
115g (4oz) caster sugar
1 tsp vanilla extract
Finely grated zest of
   1 small lemon
130g (4½oz) wheat-
   and gluten-free
   self-raising flour
Pinch of salt
1 tsp xanthan gum
1 tsp gluten-free
   baking powder
60g (2¼oz) dairy-free
   spread, melted and cooled
1 punnet of evenly
   sized strawberries
200g (7oz) marzipan
Green or blue food colouring
A few redcurrants or other
   fruit, for decoration

ingredients continue...

This French classic is a beautiful summery cake. It is so pretty and, with its kirsch-soaked sponge, tart strawberries and vanilla mousseline, completely delicious. Please don't be put off by the length of the recipe, the mousseline can be made in advance and stored in the fridge overnight, leaving you with just the sponges to bake and the strawberries to prepare. It really is worth the effort.

* First, make the crème mousseline. In a large bowl and using a large balloon whisk, beat the egg yolks until smooth.

* Combine the sugar, salt and cornflour in a heavy-based saucepan over a medium heat and slowly pour in the milk in a steady stream, stirring constantly. Cook until the mixture thickens and begins to bubble, which should take between 5 and 8 minutes.

* Once the mixture has thickened, slowly pour a third into the egg yolks, whisk to combine, then slowly pour back into the saucepan. Continue to cook over the medium heat, stirring constantly, for 5 to 10 minutes until the mixture comes to a full boil. This is very important because if the mixture doesn't boil properly, the cream won't thicken. Once the mixture is thick enough to hold its shape, remove from the heat and whisk in the vanilla extract.

* Strain the mixture through a fine sieve into a heatproof bowl. Cover with clingfilm, making sure it is pressed onto the cream to prevent a skin forming.

* Once the cream has cooled to room temperature and using a hand-held electric mixer on a high speed setting, beat in the dairy-free spread in three or four additions, making sure it is well whipped in each time. Pop into the fridge for a couple of hours to chill and firm.

* Preheat the oven to 180°C/160°C fan/Gas 4. Grease and line the base of the sandwich tins.

* In a large mixing bowl, use a hand-held electric mixer on a high setting to whisk the egg yolks and sugar together for about 5 minutes until the mixture drips like a ribbon. Add the vanilla extract and lemon zest and beat again to incorporate.

* Sift the flour, salt, xanthan gum and baking powder together and gently fold into the egg mixture.

recipe continues...

for the crème mousseline
4 large egg yolks
100g (3½oz) caster sugar
Pinch of salt
30g (1oz) cornflour
425ml (15fl oz) soya milk
¾ tsp vanilla extract
100g (3½oz) dairy-free spread

for the kirsch syrup
1 tbsp caster sugar
4 tbsp kirsch

equipment
2 x 20cm (8 inch) sandwich
  tins and 1 x 20cm (8 inch)
  deep round tin

....

tip: If you prefer, you can
make a single sponge in a
20cm (8 inch) deep round
cake tin and carefully cut it
in half. The cake would also
look stunning baked in a
20cm (8 inch) deep square
cake tin.

* Whisk the egg whites until they are stiff and fluffy, then gradually fold into the flour mixture. Gently fold in the melted dairy-free spread, trying to mix as little as possible.

* Spoon the mixture into the two sandwich tins, smoothing to the edge with the back of a dessert spoon. To make sure both cakes are the same size, I weigh the two filled tins, adjusting if necessary.

* Bake for 30 to 40 minutes or until the cakes are golden and a metal skewer inserted into the cakes comes out clean. Remove from the oven and cool in the tins for 10 minutes before turning them out onto a metal cooling rack. Leave the paper bases on the cakes until completely cooled (this will stop the sponges from shrinking).

* Now make the syrup by boiling the sugar and 200ml (7fl oz) water together in a heavy-based saucepan over a medium heat for a couple of minutes. Remove from the heat and allow to cool before stirring in the kirsch.

* Remove the baking parchment from the bottom of the cooled cakes and trim the outer crusty edges off.

* Place one cake in the bottom of the deep round cake tin with the base removed. Set a foil cake board underneath it.

* Using a pastry brush, brush the cake with half the syrup. Don't worry if it seems like too much syrup; I can assure you the cake will soak it up.

* Spoon a thin layer of the chilled crème mousseline over the sponge, spreading it evenly right to the edges. Cut all your strawberries except one in half and neatly trim the stem end, then place them in a single layer around the edge of the sponge, with the cut half facing the side of the cake tin. Fill the rest of the cake with the remaining strawberry halves. Spread the rest of your crème mousseline over the strawberries, filling in any gaps.

* Take the other cake, brush the bottom with the remaining kirsch syrup, then place it on top of the strawberries and crème inside the cake ring and gently press down.

* Colour the marzipan using only a drop of food colouring at a time and working it in gradually with your hands. You want to achieve a pale and delicate shade. On a surface dusted with a little icing sugar, roll out the marzipan to 3mm (⅛ inch) and cut around the base of your deep round cake tin. Lay it on top of the cake and smooth it out.

* Cover the cake with clingfilm and put in the fridge for a minimum of 1 hour. When you remove it from the fridge, decorate with the reserved strawberry cut in half and a few redcurrants if you can find them. (In fact, you can use whatever you like, but just remember to keep it simple.) Gently remove the cake ring and serve.

Dundee cake

serves: 12
preparation: 25 minutes
baking: 2¼ hours
cooling: 50 minutes
freeze: Yes

175g (6oz) dairy-free spread
175g (6oz) caster sugar
Finely grated zest of
    1 lemon or 1 orange
3 large eggs, beaten
1 to 2 tbsp soya/rice/
    almond milk
200g (7oz) wheat- and
    gluten-free plain flour
1 tsp xanthan gum
1 tsp gluten-free
    baking powder
50g (2oz) ground almonds
125g (4½oz) sultanas
125g (4½oz) currants
50g (2oz) candied peel
50g (2oz) glacé cherries,
    rinsed and chopped
    into quarters
50g (2oz) whole
    blanched almonds

equipment
18cm (7 inch) deep round
    cake tin

I once asked a very special oncologist what cake helped to make him so brilliant. His reply was Dundee cake! Dr Elyan, this cake is for you.

* Preheat the oven to 170°C/150°C fan/Gas 3. Grease and line the base and sides of the tin with baking parchment.

* Using a hand-held electric mixer on a high setting, cream the dairy-free spread, sugar and lemon/orange zest together in a large mixing bowl for about 3 minutes until light and fluffy.

* Gradually add the eggs and milk on a medium speed setting, mixing well between each addition. Don't worry if it curdles slightly; just turn the mixer setting to high for a couple of seconds and the mixture will become smooth again.

* Fold in the sifted flour, xanthan gum, baking powder and ground almonds using a large metal spoon so you don't knock the air out. Carefully fold in the sultanas, currants, candied peel and chopped cherries.

* Spoon the mixture into the prepared tin, levelling with the back of a dessert spoon, and make a small dip in the centre. Arrange the blanched almonds in a circular pattern round the surface of the cake. Don't push the nuts into the mixture, otherwise they will sink on baking.

* Bake for 2 to 2¼ hours, covering with baking parchment or foil if the top starts to brown too much. Insert a metal skewer into the middle of the cake – it will come out clean if the cake is cooked. Cool in the tin for 30 minutes, then remove and finish cooling on a metal cooling rack. The cake will keep well in an airtight container for up to 1 month.

tip: This is one of those cakes that benefits from being left wrapped in parchment and in an airtight tin for a few days before eating. If you bake it midweek, it will be perfect for the weekend. If stored properly, it will last for ages (that is, if the hungry hordes don't demolish it the first weekend)!

Black Forest
chocolate roulade

serves: **8 to 10**
preparation: **30 minutes**
baking: **15 minutes**
cooling: **Minimum of 3 hours, but best left overnight**
freeze: **No**

for the cake mixture
175g (6oz) good-quality (60% cocoa) dark dairy-free chocolate
½ tsp vanilla extract
6 large eggs, separated
175g (6oz) caster sugar
Icing sugar, for dusting

for the black cherry filling
6 tsp kirsch
240g (8oz) black cherry jam
1 x Dairy-free Cream (see page 170)

equipment
33cm x 23cm (13 x 9 inch) Swiss roll tin

tip: As an alternative to kirsch and cherries, the roulade works beautifully with the sharpness of raspberry jam and dairy-free cream.

A 70s throwback that is still absolutely delicious. Although I have used black cherry jam in this recipe, you could use pitted dark Morello cherries for a more tart taste – either work really well.

* Preheat the oven to 180°C/160°C fan/Gas 4. Grease and line the Swiss roll tin with baking parchment.

* Melt the chocolate, vanilla extract and 2 tbsp hot water in a heatproof bowl set over a simmering pan of water. Once melted, remove from the heat and allow to cool slightly.

* Using a hand-held electric mixer on a high setting, cream the egg yolks and sugar together in a large mixing bowl until thick and creamy. Stir in the melted chocolate.

* In a separate bowl and using a hand-held electric mixer on a high speed setting, whisk the egg whites until they make soft peaks. Fold the whisked egg whites into the chocolate mixture.

* Pour the mixture into the prepared tin and level with the back of a dessert spoon. Make sure you spread evenly right into the edges.

* Bake in the oven for 15 minutes until just risen and just firm. Remove from the oven and cover with a piece of baking parchment, then place a damp tea towel over the top. Leave to cool for a minimum of 3 hours, but preferably overnight.

* Dust another piece of baking parchment with icing sugar and carefully turn out the roulade. Peel off the parchment.

* Sprinkle the roulade with kirsch and spread the black cherry jam evenly over the top, stopping about 2.5cm (1 inch) from the far end, otherwise the filling will be squeezed out when you roll the roulade up. Spread the dairy-free cream over the top of the jam.

* Using the baking parchment to help, roll up the roulade tightly from the short end nearest to you. Make sure you end up with the join underneath and don't worry about the splits and cracks.

* Put the roulade in the fridge, wrapped in the parchment, for two hours. Unwrap and dust with icing sugar to serve. The roulade is best eaten the day it is baked, but can be stored in the fridge overnight.

Lemon loaf

makes: **12 slices**
preparation: **25 minutes**
baking: **1 hour 10 minutes**
cooling: **50 minutes**
freeze: **No**

for the cake mixture
80g (3oz) dairy-free spread
300g (10½oz) caster sugar
Finely grated zest of
    3 lemons
5 large eggs, beaten
140ml (5fl oz) soya
    double cream
240g (8oz) wheat- and
    gluten-free plain flour
1 tsp xanthan gum
½ tsp gluten-free
    baking powder
Pinch of salt

for the apricot glaze
100g (3½oz) apricot jam
150g (5½oz) icing sugar
3 tbsp lemon juice
Finely grated zest of
    1 lemon

equipment
900g (2lb) loaf tin and
    a sugar thermometer

tip: If the lemon glaze is heated over 35°C (95°F), it will recrystallize and lose its shine and crispness.

A simple lemon loaf can be elevated to greatness by a crisp and zesty glaze. If you aren't keen on lemons, you could always substitute with oranges, limes or grapefruit – they all work beautifully.

* Preheat the oven to 180°C/160°C fan/Gas 4. Grease and line the loaf tin, leaving enough lining paper hanging over the edge so you can easily lift the cake out of the tin.

* Using a hand-held electric mixer on a high setting, cream the dairy-free spread, sugar and lemon zest together for about 3 minutes in a large mixing bowl until light and fluffy.

* Gradually add the eggs and the soya cream on a medium speed setting, mixing well between each addition. Don't worry if it curdles slightly; just turn the mixer setting to high for a couple of seconds and the mixture will become smooth again.

* Fold in the sifted flour, xanthan gum, baking powder and salt using a large metal spoon so you don't knock the air out. Spoon the mixture into the loaf tin, smoothing to the edge with the back of a dessert spoon.

* Bake in the oven for 1 hour 10 minutes, turning the tin round halfway through cooking. To test if the cake is cooked, insert a metal skewer into the middle. If it comes out clean, the loaf is cooked.

* Remove the cake from the oven, immediately turning it out onto the metal cooling rack. Don't leave to cool in the tin and don't turn the oven off. After 10 minutes, place a lined baking sheet under the rack.

* To glaze the cake, lightly brush the cake all over with warmed apricot jam. Leave for 5 minutes.

* In a small heavy-based saucepan, mix the icing sugar, lemon juice and lemon zest and warm over a low heat. Clip the sugar thermometer to the inside of the saucepan to check when the icing reaches 35°C (95°F). Do not let the icing get any hotter.

* Remove from the heat and brush the lemon icing evenly over the top and sides of the cake. Leave to stand for 5 minutes to set.

* Place the cake on a baking sheet into the oven, turn off the heat and leave for 5 minutes for the glaze to dry. It should become translucent. Remove from the oven and allow to cool before slicing. Store in an airtight container for three days.

Coconut & lime cake

serves: **8 to 10**
preparation: **25 minutes**
baking: **25 minutes**
cooling: **1 hour**
freeze: **No**

for the cake mixture
175g (6oz) dairy-free spread
175g (6oz) caster sugar
3 large eggs, beaten
175g (6oz) wheat- and gluten-
free self-raising flour
1 tsp xanthan gum
1½ tsp gluten-free
baking powder
50g (2oz) desiccated coconut
2 tbsp coconut cream

for the lime filling & icing
3 limes
225g (8oz) icing sugar

equipment
2 x 20cm (8 inch)
sandwich tins

A pretty cake evocative of lazy summer days and picnics in the garden. The coconut flavour is not overpowering and friends who don't normally like coconut love this cake.

* Preheat the oven to 180°C/160°C fan/Gas 4. Grease the sandwich tins, then line the bases with baking parchment.

* Using a hand-held electric mixer on a high speed setting, cream the dairy-free spread and caster sugar together.

* Gradually add the beaten eggs on a medium speed setting, mixing well between each addition. Don't worry if the mixture curdles slightly; just turn the mixer setting up to high for a couple of seconds and the mixture will become smooth again.

* Fold in the sifted flour, xanthan gum and baking powder using a large metal spoon so you don't knock the air out. Add the desiccated coconut and coconut cream, carefully folding in until combined.

* Spoon the mixture into the two sandwich tins, smoothing to the edge with the back of a dessert spoon. To make sure both cakes are the same size, I weigh the two filled tins, adjusting if necessary.

* Bake for 25 minutes or until the cakes begin to shrink away from the sides of the tin and are evenly golden brown in colour.

* Whilst the cakes are baking, you can make up the filling and icing. Remove the zest from the limes with a zester, which will give you nice long and curly strips that will look pretty as decoration on the cake.

* Cut the limes in half and, with a small sharp knife, remove all the outer pith. Over a bowl, use the knife to prepare the half limes like a grapefruit. Insert the blade, running it around the edge between the fruit and skin. Then slide the knife blade in between each membrane and segment, scooping the segments out into the bowl.

* Sift the icing sugar on top of the lime segments and captured juice, a little at a time. Carefully fold in with a tablespoon so you don't break up the segments too much. When all the sugar has been folded in, allow the mixture to rest for 5 minutes.

* Remove the baked cakes from the oven, leaving them to cool in their tins for 10 minutes. Carefully turn the cakes out, removing the baking parchment, and leave to cool on a metal cooling rack.

recipe continues...

tip: Don't use all the lime juice, or your filling/icing will be far too runny. Only use the juice that dribbles out as you release the segments. You can always add more juice if the icing is too stiff.

* When the cakes are cold, place one cake upside down on a cake board or serving plate. Spread half of the filling/icing over the surface of this cake. Carefully place the other cake on top.

* Spread the remaining icing over the top of the cake with a round-bladed knife or a palette knife, taking the icing to the edge. Sprinkle the lime zest over the top to decorate.

* Place the cake in the fridge for 30 minutes to firm the icing, but don't leave it any longer, otherwise the sponge will begin to harden.

Chocolate
& almond sponge

serves: 8 to 10
preparation: 30 minutes
baking: 20 minutes
cooling: 30 minutes
freeze: Yes

for the cake mixture
250g (9oz) dairy-free spread
250g (9oz) caster sugar
250g (9oz) eggs, beaten
    (about 4 eggs)
2 tbsp soya/rice/almond milk
1 tsp vanilla extract
170g (6oz) wheat and gluten-
    free self-raising flour
50g (2oz) cocoa powder
1 tsp xanthan gum
1½ tsp gluten-free
    baking powder

ingredients continue...

I love this simple moist and chocolaty sponge cake and it's remarkably versatile. It can be dressed up with a layer of chocolate icing on top and pale pink roses or jazzed up with a fudgy frosting and bright decorations for a fun and funky children's birthday cake.

* Preheat the oven to 190°C/170°C fan/Gas 5. Grease the tins and line the bases with baking parchment.

* Using a hand-held electric mixer on a high speed setting, cream the dairy-free spread and sugar together for about 3 minutes until light and fluffy.

* Beat the eggs, milk and vanilla extract together in a small bowl. Gradually add the beaten eggs mixture to the spread and sugar on a medium setting, mixing well between each addition. Don't worry if the mixture curdles slightly; just turn the mixer setting up to high for a couple of seconds and the mixture will become smooth again.

* Fold in the sifted flour, cocoa powder, xanthan gum, baking powder and ground almonds using a large metal spoon so you don't knock the air out.

* Spoon the mixture into the two sandwich tins, smoothing to the edge with the back of a dessert spoon. To make sure both cakes are the same size, I weigh the two filled tins, adjusting if necessary.

recipe continues...

30g (1oz) ground almonds
½ tbsp cocoa powder,
    for dusting

for the chocolate filling
55g (2oz) good-quality
    (60% cocoa) dark dairy-
    free chocolate
55g (2oz) dairy-free spread
2 tbsp soya/rice/almond milk
½ tsp vanilla extract
185g (6½oz) icing sugar

equipment
2 x 20cm (8 inch)
    sandwich tins

....

* Bake for 20 minutes or until the cakes begin to shrink away from the sides of the tins and are firm to the touch.

* Whilst the cakes are baking, you can make the filling. Gently heat the chocolate in a heatproof bowl set over a pan of simmering water for about 10 minutes, or until the chocolate has just melted, stirring occasionally. Don't let the bottom of the bowl touch the water. If you have a microwave, you can place the chocolate in a heatproof bowl and heat for 1 minute. Remove and stir the chocolate until it has completely melted.

* Using a hand-held mixer on a high setting, cream the dairy-free spread and milk together until smooth. Stir in the melted chocolate and vanilla. Beat in the icing sugar until thick and creamy, adding more milk if required. Remember that the icing will firm up as the chocolate begins to set, so it is better for the icing to initially be slightly loose.

* Remove the baked cakes from the oven and cool in the tins for 10 minutes before turning them onto a metal cooling rack. Leave the paper bases on the cakes until completely cooled, as this will stop the sponges from shrinking.

* Place one cake upside down on a cake board or serving plate. Spread the chocolate filling right to the edge of the base cake, and then carefully place the other cake on top. Dust with cocoa powder to serve.

tip: If you are allergic to nuts, or just don't like them, remove the ground almonds and increase the flour to 250g (9oz). The cake will still be lovely and moist, but not quite so rich.

Moist orange
& almond cake

serves: **8 to 10**
preparation: **3 hours to boil the oranges + 20 minutes**
baking: **1 hour**
cooling: **30 minutes**
freeze: **Yes**

2 oranges
6 medium eggs
225g (8oz) caster sugar
225g (8oz) ground almonds
1 tsp gluten-free
   baking powder
Icing sugar, for dusting

equipment
23cm (9 inch) springform
   sandwich tin

Often referred to as Passover cake, this wonderfully moist Middle Eastern-inspired cake is perfect for those of us on a restricted diet, as it doesn't contain flour or butter. I first discovered it years ago when planning a dinner party for friends. I wanted a dessert that could be made in advance and one that was fruity and light. I served it warm with fresh berries and ice cream and it was an instant hit, quickly passing into my repertoire of favourite desserts.

* Put the whole oranges into a heavy-based saucepan with lots of water. Bring to the boil, cover with a lid and boil gently for 3 hours, topping up the water when necessary. Drain and leave to cool.

* Once cool, break the oranges open and remove the stalks and any pips. Put the flesh into a food processor and blend to a purée. Put to one side.

* Preheat the oven to 180°C/160°C fan/Gas 4. Grease and line the cake tin with baking parchment.

* In a large mixing bowl, use a hand-held electric mixer on a high speed setting to whisk together the eggs and sugar until thick and moussey. The mixture should leave a trail over the surface.

* Fold in the ground almonds, baking powder and orange purée.

* Pour the mixture into the prepared tin and bake for 55 minutes to 1 hour or until a metal skewer inserted into the middle of the cake comes out clean.

* Remove from the oven and leave to cool in the tin for 10 minutes. Gently remove from the tin, carefully take off the baking parchment and leave to cool on a metal cooling rack.

* Dust with icing sugar to serve. The cake can be stored in an airtight container for up to three days.

Hummingbird cake

serves: 14 to 16
preparation: 30 minutes
baking: 30 minutes
cooling: 45 minutes
freeze: No

for the cake mixture

- 80g (3oz) pecans or walnuts, toasted and chopped
- 50g (2oz) coconut flakes
- 225g (8oz) tin of crushed pineapple in fruit juice (or chopped pineapple whizzed into a paste in a food processor)
- 250g (9oz) wheat- and gluten-free self-raising flour
- 1 tsp xanthan gum
- 1 tsp gluten-free baking powder
- 1 tsp cinnamon
- 225g (8oz) caster sugar
- A pinch of salt
- 2 very ripe bananas, mashed
- 150ml (5fl oz) sunflower oil
- 3 large eggs, beaten
- 1 tsp vanilla extract

for the frosting

- 1 large egg white
- 175g (6oz) caster sugar
- ¼ tsp cream of tartar

equipment

- 2 x 20cm (8 inch) sandwich tins

The American Magazine Southern Living *is generally credited with the first reference to the Hummingbird cake. It published the recipe submitted by Mrs L H Wiggins in 1978, but Mrs Wiggins didn't give any details of the cake's origins, so it remains a bit of a mystery. Could it be because the hummingbird is a symbol of sweetness? Whatever its origins, this traditional Southern cake is a bit of a showstopper.*

* Preheat the oven to 195°C/175°C fan/Gas 5. Grease the two tins and then line the bases with baking parchment.

* Toast all the pecans or walnuts by spreading them out on a baking sheet and placing in the oven for 7 to 8 minutes. Once toasted, chop and put to one side.

* At the same time on another baking sheet, spread out the coconut flakes and toast for 5 minutes. Remove from the oven and put to one side.

* Drain the pineapple and reserve the juice.

* In a large mixing bowl, combine the flour, xanthan gum, baking powder, cinnamon, sugar and salt and make a well in the centre. Add the crushed pineapple with 4 tablespoons of the juice, the mashed bananas, sunflower oil, toasted pecans or walnuts, eggs and vanilla extract. Using a large balloon whisk, beat for 1 minute or until smooth.

* Spoon the mixture into the two sandwich tins, smoothing to the edge with the back of a dessert spoon. To make sure both cakes are the same size, I weigh the two filled tins, adjusting if necessary.

* Bake in the oven for 25 to 30 minutes or until the cakes are well risen, golden and the sponges spring back when touched. You will also find that the sponges shrink from the sides of the tin once the cakes are cooked.

* Remove the baked cakes from the oven and cool in the tins for 10 minutes before turning them onto a metal cooling rack. Leave the paper bases on the cakes until completely cooled, as this will stop the sponges from shrinking.

recipe continues...

* Whilst the cakes are cooling, make the frosting. Measure all the ingredients and 2 tbsp water into a heatproof bowl over a saucepan of hot water and, using a hand-held electric mixer on a medium speed setting, whisk for 10 to 12 minutes or until thick.

* Place one cake on a cake board or serving plate and spread a little of the frosting evenly over the surface, then carefully place the other sponge on top and press down lightly to join the two.

* Working quickly as the icing sets rapidly, use the remainder of the frosting to cover the top and sides of the cake, swirling the icing to form soft peaks. Sprinkle the top and sides of the cake with the toasted coconut flakes.

* Leave the cake to set in a cool place, but not the fridge, before serving. Store in an airtight container for up to two days.

Traybakes

White chocolate
& peanut butter blondies

makes: **12 small squares**
preparation: **20 minutes**
baking: **30 minutes**
cooling: **30 minutes**
freeze: **Yes**

100g (3½oz) dairy-free spread
150g (5½oz) crunchy
   peanut butter
175g (6oz) soft light
   brown sugar
1 large egg, beaten
1 tsp vanilla extract
125g (4½oz) wheat- and
   gluten-free plain flour
1 tsp xathan gum
1 tsp gluten-free
   baking powder
75g (2¾oz) white dairy-
   free chocolate drops
   (or chopped chocolate)

equipment
20cm (8 inch) square tin

As much as I love brownies, sometimes I feel like a change and these little blondies are to die for. My son Charlie and his chums love them, so I always put some aside to enjoy on my own in peace!

* Preheat the oven to 170°C/150°C fan/Gas 3. Grease and line the baking tin, leaving enough baking parchment hanging over the edge so you can easily lift out the blondies.

* Using a hand-held electric mixer on a high speed setting, beat the dairy-free spread and peanut butter together for about 3 minutes until nice and soft. Add the sugar, egg and vanilla extract and beat until well combined.

* Gradually fold in the flour, xanthan gum and baking powder using a large metal spoon. Fold in the drops or chopped pieces of white chocolate until evenly distributed through the dough-like mixture. Spoon the mixture into the prepared baking tin, spreading evenly with the back of a dessert spoon.

* Bake for 25 to 30 minutes or until golden brown in colour and firm to the touch. Remove from the oven and leave to cool in the tin. Once cool, remove from the tin and cut into squares.

Sticky toffee traybake

makes: 16 squares
preparation: 30 minutes
baking: 50 minutes
cooling: 30 minutes
freeze: Yes

200g (7oz) dairy-free spread
200g (7oz) golden syrup
200g (7oz) light
    muscovado sugar
200g (7oz) wheat- and gluten-
    free self-raising flour
1 tsp xanthan gum
100g (3½oz) ground
    almonds
1 tsp salt
3 large eggs, beaten
2 tbsp soya/rice/
    almond milk
225g (8oz) marzipan
Food colourings,
    for decoration
Icing sugar or edible glitter,
    for decoration

equipment
18 x 27cm (7 x 10½ inch)
    shallow baking tin

Totally addictive and Charlie's all-time favourite cake. Yummy, moist, toffee-flavoured sponge with a lovely sticky surface and topped with marzipan. A brilliant cake for children's parties.

* Preheat the oven to 160°C/140°C fan/Gas 3. Grease and line the baking tin with baking parchment, leaving a couple of centimetres (about 1 inch) over at the ends to help lift the traybake out of the pan when baked.

* Gently melt the dairy-free spread and golden syrup in a heavy-based saucepan over a low heat, stirring to combine. When melted, remove from the heat and put to one side to cool.

* Place the muscovado sugar into a large mixing bowl. Sift the flour, xanthan gum, ground almonds and salt into the muscovado sugar, breaking up any large lumps that may form.

* Using a large balloon whisk, beat in the cooled syrup mixture, stirring until combined. Stir in the beaten eggs and milk, whisking until combined into a nice heavy batter.

* Pour the batter into the baking tin. Bake for 50 minutes or until the sponge has risen beautifully and a metal skewer inserted into the middle of the cake comes out clean. Remove from the oven and leave in the tin to cool. Once cool, remove from the tin and cut into squares.

* Colour your marzipan with food colours of your choice, then roll out, dusting the surface with icing sugar, and cut into desired shapes. Place on top of the squares. Dust with icing sugar or edible glitter.

tip: I use stars or daisies on my traybake, but any small shape would work well. Little teddies, fish and butterflies are particularly fun and funky for children.

Cake angels
chocolate brownies

makes: **12 to 16 squares**
preparation: **20 minutes**
baking: **30 minutes**
cooling: **1 hour**
freeze: **Yes**

200g (7oz) good-quality
(60% cocoa) dark dairy-
free chocolate
200g (7oz) dairy-free butter
2 large eggs, beaten
1 medium egg, beaten
300g (10½oz) caster sugar
1½ tsp vanilla extract
100g (3½oz) wheat- and
gluten-free plain flour
1 tsp xanthan gum
½ tsp salt
35g (1¼oz) cocoa powder,
plus extra for dusting

equipment
18 x 27cm (7 x 10½ inch)
shallow baking tin

tip: If you can bear to leave
them, the brownies taste
even better the day after
baking. They are delicious
on their own with a cup
of coffee, or serve warm
with raspberry coulis and
dairy-free ice cream.

'Exquisite', 'rich', 'fudgy' and 'totally delicious' are just some of the words that have been used to describe my award-winning brownies. The key is to use really good quality dairy-free chocolate with a minimum of 60% cocoa solids. I can guarantee that no one will know they are dairy-, wheat- and gluten-free.

* Preheat the oven to 160°C/140°C fan/Gas 3. Grease and line the baking tin, leaving enough baking parchment hanging over the edge so you can lift the brownies easily out of the tin.

* Melt the chocolate and dairy-free spread together in a heatproof bowl. You can either do this over a simmering pan of water on the stove, making sure the bottom of the bowl does not touch the water, or microwave on a high setting for about 1½ minutes. Stir to make sure the ingredients have melted together.

* Using a hand-held electric mixer on a high speed setting, beat the eggs, sugar and vanilla together for about 5 minutes until it becomes thick, creamy and pale in colour.

* Gradually add the melted chocolate and dairy-free spread, using a slow mixer speed, until the mixture is well combined. Gently fold the sifted flour, xanthan gum, salt and cocoa powder through the creamy mixture using long, folding motions (you don't want to beat the air out). Spoon the mixture into the lined baking tin, making sure it is evenly distributed, and level with the back of a metal spoon.

* Bake for 30 minutes. You might think they don't look cooked and be tempted to leave them in for longer, but don't. Brownies continue to cook and firm up as they cool.

* Leave the brownies to cool in the tin for 1 hour, if you can last that long! They will be easier to cut the longer you leave them. Dust lightly with cocoa powder. Remove the brownies from the tin, peel off the baking parchment and leave to finish cooling on a metal cooling rack.

* Once cold, cut into squares using a large plastic knife if you have one. If you don't, use a large sharp knife heated in hot water between slices. It will stop you getting into a lovely gooey mess.

Lemon polenta traybake

makes: **16 squares**
preparation: **20 minutes**
baking: **30 minutes**
cooling: **30 minutes**
freeze: **Yes**

for the traybake mixture
175g (6oz) dairy-free spread
175g (6oz) caster sugar
3 medium eggs, beaten
150g (5½oz) fine polenta
**100g (3½oz) ground
    almonds**
1 tsp vanilla extract
**2 tsp gluten-free
    baking powder**

for the lemon syrup
50g (2oz) granulated sugar
Zest and juice of 1 lemon

equipment
**18 x 27cm (7 x 10½ inch)
    shallow baking tin**

I use fine polenta in this zesty traybake, but if you prefer a crunchier texture, coarse polenta works just as well.

* Preheat the oven to 180°C/160°C fan/Gas 4. Grease and line the baking tin with baking parchment, leaving a couple of centimetres (about 1 inch) over at the ends to help lift the traybake out of the pan when baked.

* Using a hand-held electric mixer on a high speed setting, cream together the dairy-free spread and sugar for about 3 minutes until light and fluffy.

* Gradually add the beaten eggs and the polenta on a medium speed setting, mixing well to combine. Fold in the ground almonds, vanilla extract and baking powder until all the ingredients are combined.

* Spoon the mixture into the baking tin and level with the back of a metal spoon. Bake for 30 minutes or until golden brown and a metal skewer inserted into the middle of the traybake comes out clean.

* Whilst the traybake is in the oven, prepare the syrup by mixing the sugar, lemon juice and lemon zest in a small mixing bowl, stirring until the sugar begins to dissolve.

* Remove the traybake from the oven and leave in the tin. Whilst the cake is still hot, drizzle the lemon syrup evenly over the top. Once cooled, remove the traybake from the tin and cut into squares.

tip: To make sure you get a crunchy, zesty topping, always drizzle the syrup over a warm/hot cake so the juice will soak in, leaving the crunchy sugar on top.

Chocolate nutty caramels

makes: **30 bars**
preparation: **40 minutes**
baking: **20 minutes**
cooling: **1 hour**
freeze: **Yes**

for the chocolate base
200g (7oz) dairy-free spread
50g (2oz) cocoa powder
300g (10½oz) dark
   brown sugar
2 large eggs, beaten
225g (8oz) wheat- and
   gluten-free plain flour
1 tsp xanthan gum

for the caramel
300g (10½oz) mixed nuts
 (hazelnuts, pistachios,
 almonds, walnuts)
175g (6oz) dairy-free spread
115g (4oz) caster sugar
3 tbsp golden syrup
400g (14oz) Dairy-free
   Condensed Milk
   (see page 167)

equipment
20cm x 30cm (8 x 12 inch)
   baking tin

When I first gave up dairy products, I realized I also couldn't have toffee or caramel. So imagine my delight when I discovered I could make dairy-free condensed milk. A whole forgotten world of sticky, gooey deliciousness suddenly opened up to me and these nutty bars were one of the first recipes I tried. Although the recipe makes 30 bars, be warned: they never seem to last long!

* Preheat the oven to 160°C/140°C fan/Gas 3. Grease and line the baking tin, leaving enough lining paper hanging over the edge so you can lift out the caramels easily.

* Toast all the nuts by spreading them out on a baking sheet and placing in the oven for 7 to 8 minutes. Remove from the oven and put to one side.

* Prepare the base. In a medium-sized heavy-based saucepan, melt the dairy-free spread over a medium heat, stir in the cocoa powder and then the sugar and stir until combined. Remove from the heat and stir in the eggs until combined.

* Stir in the sifted flour and xanthan gum. Spoon the mixture into the lined baking tin, making sure it is evenly distributed, and level with the back of a metal spoon.

* Bake in the oven for 20 minutes or until firm to the touch. Remove from the oven and leave to cool.

* To make the nutty caramel, place the dairy-free spread, sugar, golden syrup and condensed milk into a medium-sized heavy-based saucepan and heat gently until the sugar has dissolved.

* Bring to the boil and simmer for 10 to 15 minutes, stirring constantly, until the mixture becomes thick and dark in colour. Remove from the heat and leave to cool for 15 minutes.

* Stir the toasted mixed nuts into the caramel and spoon evenly over the cooled chocolate base. Place in the fridge to chill until firm.

* Cut into bars with a sharp knife and store in an airtight container in the fridge for up to seven days.

tip: Don't let the caramel burn, as it will taste horrid and make a real mess. Stir constantly and if, like me, you get bored, read a book whilst you are doing it!

Date & walnut traybake

My version is based on the late Queen Mother's favourite cake and is one of my most popular traybakes. It is wonderfully moist and sticky with a lovely crunchy top and keeps very well if stored in an airtight tin. If you prefer, you can always make this as a 20cm (8 inch) round cake, which will serve eight to ten people.

makes: 16 squares
preparation: 20 minutes
baking: 40 minutes
cooling: 30 minutes
freeze: Yes

for the traybake mixture
200g (7oz) chopped dates
1 tsp bicarbonate of soda
85g (3oz) dairy-free spread
200g (7oz) soft light
   brown sugar
1 large egg, beaten
1 tsp vanilla extract
150g (5½oz) wheat- and
   gluten-free plain flour
1 tsp xanthan gum
½ tsp salt
100g (3½oz) ground
   almonds
1 tsp gluten free
   baking powder
50g (2oz) chopped walnuts

for the topping
5 tbsp soft light brown sugar
2 tbsp dairy-free spread
2 tbsp soya double cream

equipment
18 x 27cm (7 x 10½ inch)
   shallow baking tin

* Preheat the oven to 170°C/150°C fan/Gas 3. Grease and line the baking tin with baking parchment, leaving a couple of centimetres (about 1 inch) over at the ends to help lift the traybake out of the pan when baked.

* Soak the chopped dates in 175ml (6fl oz) boiling water with the bicarbonate of soda and put to one side whilst mixing the other ingredients.

* Place the dairy-free spread, light brown sugar, beaten egg, vanilla extract, flour, xanthan gum, salt, ground almonds and baking powder into a large mixing bowl and stir with a large metal spoon until combined. Add the soaked dates and liquid to the mixture and stir until combined.

* Spoon the mixture into the baking tin and level with the back of a metal spoon. Bake for 40 minutes or until a metal skewer inserted into the traybake comes out clean. Remove the traybake from the oven and leave to cool in the tin.

* Whilst the cake is cooling, you can make the topping. In a heavy-based saucepan, mix together the light brown sugar, dairy-free spread and cream, bring to the boil and continue to boil for 3 minutes. Remove from the heat and leave to cool for 5 minutes.

* Remove the traybake from the tin and remove the baking parchment. Slowly spoon the toffee topping over the surface (it doesn't matter if it dribbles down the sides). Sprinkle the chopped walnuts over the top of the traybake and cut into squares.

tip: You can save time by buying pre-chopped dates and walnuts.

Flapjacks

makes: 25 to 30 slices
preparation: 20 minutes
baking: 30 minutes
cooling: 20 minutes
freeze: Yes

340g (11½oz) light
   muscovado sugar
300g (10½oz) dairy-free
   spread
4 generous tbsp golden syrup
200g (7oz) Dairy-free
   Condensed Milk
   (see page 167)
500g (1lb 2oz) gluten-
   free porridge oats (see Key
   Ingredients, page 10)

equipment
25 x 38cm (10 x 15 inch)
   Swiss roll tin or
   roasting tin

I have spent years trying to find the perfect flapjack recipe, one that produces lovely chewy flapjacks with a hint of caramel, not hard and floury ones that fall apart when you eat them. This recipe gets the thumbs-up from Charlie and all his friends, and I think it is pretty perfect as well. Don't forget to use gluten-free oats, which you can buy from supermarkets.

* Preheat the oven to 180°C/160°C fan/Gas 4. Grease and line the tin with baking parchment, leaving a couple of centimetres (about 1 inch) over at the ends to help lift the flapjacks out of the pan when baked.

* Melt the sugar, dairy-free spread and syrup over a medium heat in a large saucepan or casserole dish, stirring to stop the mixture from catching. Make sure the dairy-free spread has melted and don't worry if the mixture separates. Remove the pan from the heat.

* Pour in the cold condensed milk and stir until combined. Pour in the oats and stir until combined. Spoon the mixture into the pan and level right to the corners with the back of a dessert spoon.

* Bake for 30 minutes or until lightly brown. Don't worry if they look a bit wobbly, they will firm up as they cool down and set. We want soft chewy flapjacks, not dry and hard ones.

* Remove from the oven and, whilst still warm, carefully remove from the tin and cut into squares or fingers. Leave to finish cooling on a metal cooling rack.

tip: To ring the changes, you could add the following ingredients:
* *fruity flapjacks* 100g (3½oz) mixture of raisins, sultanas, dates and dried apricots
* *ginger flapjacks* 75g (2¾oz) finely chopped glacé ginger
* *flapjacks with seeds* 75g (2¾oz) sunflower, sesame or pumpkin seeds

Harry's brownies

makes: 16 squares
preparation: 20 minutes
baking: 50 minutes
cooling: 30 minutes
freeze: Yes

225g (8oz) dairy-free spread
400g (14oz) caster sugar
3 large eggs, beaten
1½ tsp vanilla extract
120g (4½oz) wheat- and
   gluten-free plain flour
1½ tsp xanthan gum
½ tsp salt
75g (2¾ oz) cocoa powder
100g (3½oz) good-quality
   (60% cocoa) dark dairy-
   free chocolate drops

equipment
18 x 27cm (7 x 10½ inch)
   shallow baking tin

tip: If your children are anything like my nephew, you will need to hide these and ration out when appropriate!

My nephew Harry just loves these brownies. They are not as rich and dense as my award-winning brownies, which is probably why they appeal so much to the younger generation, but the scattered chocolates drops give them a wonderful bite that is quite addictive.

* Preheat the oven to 180°C/160°C fan/Gas 4. Grease and line the baking tin with baking parchment, leaving a couple of centimetres (about 1 inch) over at the ends to help lift the brownies out of the pan when baked.

* Using a hand-held electric mixer on a high speed setting, cream together the dairy-free spread and sugar for about 3 minutes until light and fluffy.

* Gradually add the beaten eggs and vanilla extract on a medium speed setting, mixing well between each addition. Don't worry if the mixture curdles slightly; just turn the mixer setting up to high for a couple of seconds and the mixture will become smooth again.

* Fold in the sifted flour, xanthan gum, salt and cocoa powder using a large metal spoon until everything is combined. Stir in three-quarters of the chocolate drops.

* Spoon the mixture into the baking tin and level with the back of a metal spoon. Sprinkle the remaining chocolate drops evenly over the mixture.

* Bake for 45 to 50 minutes. The brownies will be ready when a metal skewer inserted into the middle of the brownies comes out slightly tacky. You don't want to overcook the brownies because they need to be soft and fudgy and will continue to firm up as they cool.

* Remove from the oven and leave to cool in the tin. Once cooled, turn out of the tin, cut into squares and enjoy.

Bakewell slice

makes: 20 slices

preparation: 20 minutes +
    30 minutes cooking time

baking: 10 minutes +
    35 minutes

cooling: 40 minutes

freeze: Yes

The combination of soft almond sponge, gooey raspberry jam and crisp pastry is a classic. It is well loved and quite rightly so – it's totally delicious.

for the pastry base
125g (4½oz) wheat- and
    gluten-free plain flour
1 tsp xanthan gum
30g (1oz) icing sugar
50g (2oz) dairy-free spread
1 large egg yolk

for the filling
120g (4½oz) dairy-free
    spread
115g (4oz) caster sugar
4 eggs, beaten
125g (4½oz) ground almonds
¼ tsp almond extract
160g (5½oz) raspberry jam

for the topping
25g (1oz) flaked almonds
75g (2¾oz) sifted icing sugar
3 tbsp boiled water

equipment
20 x 30cm (8 x 12 inch)
    shallow baking tin

tip: Also delicious using strawberry, apricot or blackcurrant jam.

* Preheat the oven to 180°C/160°C fan/Gas 4. Grease and line the tin with baking parchment, leaving a couple of centimetres (about 1 inch) over at the ends to help lift the Bakewell slice out of the pan when baked.

* To make the pastry base, sift the flour, xanthan gum and icing sugar into a mixing bowl. Add the dairy-free spread and rub in until the mixture looks like fine breadcrumbs. Add the egg yolk and 2 tablespoons cold water and mix together with a flat-bladed knife until the mixture comes together in beads. Gather into a ball, cover with clingfilm and pop in the fridge for 30 minutes.

* Remove from the fridge and roll out between two sheets of baking parchment (this prevents the pastry sticking to your rolling pin). Place the rolled-out pastry into the baking tin, pressing gently into the corners.

* Bake for 10 minutes, remove from the oven and leave to cool.

* Using a hand-held electric mixer on a high setting, make the sponge filling by beating the dairy-free spread with the caster sugar for about 3 minutes until light and fluffy.

* Gradually beat in the eggs on a medium speed setting. Don't worry if the mixture curdles slightly; just turn the mixer up to high for a few seconds and the mixture will become smooth again. Fold in the ground almonds and almond extract until combined.

* Spread the jam over the pastry base, making sure to smooth to the edges. Spoon the sponge filling over the jam, levelling into the corners with the back of a dessert spoon. Sprinkle with the flaked almonds.

* Bake for 30 to 35 minutes or until firm to the touch and golden brown. Remove from the oven and leave to cool in the tin. When cooled, remove from the tin.

* Mix the sifted icing sugar with 2 to 3 tablespoons of just boiled water to make a runny paste. Drizzle over the Bakewell slice in a zigzag pattern and leave to set before cutting into squares.

Sticky gingerbread

makes: **16 squares**
preparation: **20 minutes**
baking: **1¼ hours**
cooling: **1 hour**
freeze: **Yes**

175g (6oz) black treacle
175g (6oz) golden syrup
175g (6oz) dark brown
   muscovado sugar
175g (6oz) dairy-free spread
350g (12oz) wheat- and
   gluten-free plain flour
2 tsp xanthan gum
½ tsp bicarbonate of soda
1 tbsp ground ginger
1 tsp ground mixed spice
150ml (5fl oz) soya/rice/
   almond milk
1 large egg, beaten
75g (2¾oz) glacé ginger

equipment
20cm (8 inch) deep square tin

I love my sticky and spicy gingerbread cut into generous squares, but traditionally it was thinly sliced and buttered, just like bread. Although I know you will be tempted to tuck in straight away, I promise it will taste even better if you leave it wrapped up in a tin for a couple of days.

* Preheat the oven to 170°C/150°C fan/Gas 3. Grease and line the cake tin.

* Place the treacle, golden syrup, sugar and dairy-free spread in a heavy-based saucepan over a gentle heat. Stir occasionally until the spread has melted and the sugar dissolved. Remove from the heat.

* Sift the flour, xanthan gum, bicarbonate of soda, ground ginger and mixed spice into a large mixing bowl and make a well in the centre.

* Slowly blend the milk into the syrup mixture – it should now be just tepid in temperature. If it is too hot, leave it to cool for a little longer.

* Gradually pour the syrup mixture into the flour, then add the egg and glacé ginger and beat with a large balloon whisk until combined. The mixture should now be smooth and shiny.

* Pour into the prepared cake tin and bake in the oven for 1 to 1¼ hours. The gingerbread should have risen and a metal skewer inserted into the middle should come out clean. If you remove it too soon, the gingerbread will deflate and dip in the middle.

* Remove from the oven and leave to cool in the tin for 1 hour before removing the baking parchment and transferring to a metal cooling rack.

* Wrap the gingerbread in fresh baking parchment and silver foil and store in an airtight container for two days before cutting into squares and serving.

* Store in an airtight container, wrapped in baking parchment and foil, for up to ten days.

Cappuccino brownies

makes: **12 to 16 squares**
preparation: **25 minutes**
baking: **40 minutes**
cooling: **1 hour 20 minutes**
freeze: **Yes**

for the brownie mixture
225g (8oz) dairy-free spread
225g (8oz) golden
    caster sugar
4 large eggs, beaten
3 tbsp instant coffee
    granules, dissolved in
    2 tbsp hot water and
    then cooled
175g (6oz) wheat- and gluten-
    free self-raising flour
1 tsp gluten-free
    baking powder
1 tsp xanthan gum
1 tsp cocoa powder, plus
    extra for dusting
50g (2oz) ground almonds

*for the white chocolate
frosting*
115g (4 oz) white dairy-
    free chocolate
55g (2oz) dairy-free spread
3 tbsp soya/rice/almond milk
275g (9¾oz) icing sugar,
    sifted

equipment
18 x 27cm (7 x 10½ inch)
    shallow baking tin

Technically these little coffee squares are not brownies, but they are so moist and irresistible that they might as well be. I'm not a great coffee fan, but I treat myself to a soya cappuccino when I am out and feel the same way about these brownies.

* Preheat the oven to 180°C/160°C fan/Gas 4. Grease and line the baking tin, leaving enough baking parchment hanging over the edge so you can lift the brownies easily out of the tin.

* To make the brownies, in a large mixing bowl use a hand-held electric mixer on a high setting to cream the dairy-free spread and sugar together for about 3 minutes until light and fluffy. Gradually add the eggs and coffee on a medium speed setting, mixing well between each addition. Don't worry if it curdles slightly; just turn the mixer speed up to high for a few seconds and the mixture will become smooth again.

* Fold in the sifted flour, baking powder, xanthan gum, cocoa powder and ground almonds using a large metal spoon so you don't knock the air out. Don't worry if the final mixture looks slightly grainy and curdled, it will be fine.

* Spoon the mixture into the baking tin, smoothing to the edges with the back of a dessert spoon. Bake for 35 to 40 minutes or until the cake is well risen and springs back when touched. Remove from the oven and leave to cool in the tin for 20 minutes.

* Once cooled, remove the brownies from the tin, peel off the baking parchment and leave to cool completely on a metal cooling rack. Whilst the brownies are cooling, make the white chocolate frosting. Place the chocolate, dairy-free spread and milk in a heatproof bowl over a pan of simmering water that has been taken off the heat. Keep stirring until the chocolate has melted and the mixture combined.

* Remove the bowl from the pan and sift in the icing sugar. Beat until smooth. The icing may appear runny, but leave it to firm up for 30 minutes before using a round-bladed knife to spread over the brownies. Dust the top of the brownies with the cocoa powder and cut into squares.

tip: White dairy-free chocolate is quite hard to handle, so don't try to melt it in the microwave. Heat the water in the saucepan to boiling, then immediately remove from the heat, placing the heatproof bowl over it. Keep stirring the chocolate and dairy-free spread until it has all melted and combined.

Parkin

makes: **12 to 16 squares**
preparation: **30 minutes**
baking: **1¼ hours**
cooling: **1 hour**
freeze: **Yes, but keeps
well anyway**

115g (4oz) golden syrup
115g (4oz) black treacle
80g (3oz) dairy-free spread
80g (3oz) soft dark
    brown sugar
115g (4oz) wheat- and gluten-
    free self-raising flour
1 tsp xanthan gum
1 tsp bicarbonate of soda
2 tsp ground ginger
½ tsp ground cinnamon
½ tsp ground nutmeg
Pinch of salt
225g (8oz) gluten-free
    porridge oats (see Key
    Ingredients, page 10)
1 egg, beaten
2 tbsp soya/rice/almond milk

equipment
18cm (7 inch) deep square tin

There is some disagreement over how long you should leave Parkin to mature. Some say two weeks, even three. I'm happy that this recipe tastes really good after a week. Wrap in baking parchment and silver foil, then store in an airtight container, but whatever you do, don't forget it!

* Preheat the oven to 150°C/130°C fan/Gas 2. Line the sides and base of the cake tin.

* In a medium-sized heavy-based saucepan over a low heat, melt the syrup, treacle, dairy-free spread and sugar. Do not allow to boil. Remove from the heat and put to one side to cool.

* Sift the flour, xanthan gum, bicarbonate of soda, spices and salt into a large mixing bowl. Stir in the oats.

* Make a well in the centre and, using a large balloon whisk, beat in the syrup mixture, egg and milk.

* Spoon the mixture into the prepared tin and bake for 1 to 1¼ hours or until firm to the touch.

* Remove from the oven and leave to cool in the tin. Don't worry if the cake sinks slightly in the middle. Remove from the tin and wrap the cake in fresh baking parchment and silver foil. Store in an airtight container for a week before cutting into squares.

Black Forest brownies

makes: **16 squares**
preparation: **30 minutes**
baking: **35 minutes**
cooling: **30 minutes**
freeze: **Yes**

225g (8oz) good-quality
  (60% cocoa) dark dairy-
  free chocolate
125g (4½oz) dairy-free spread
3 tbsp soya double cream
3 large eggs, beaten
225g (8oz) caster sugar
2 tbsp kirsch or kirsch syrup
  from a jar of cherries
160g (5½oz) wheat- and
  gluten-free plain flour
1 tsp xanthan gum
100g (3½oz) good-quality
  (60% cocoa) dark dairy-
  free chocolate drops
  (or chopped chocolate)
450g (1lb) jar of black
  cherries in kirsch
  (175g/6oz drained weight)

equipment
8 x 27cm (7 x 10½ inch)
  shallow baking tin

These brownies not only taste great eaten cold with a cup of coffee, they also make a deliciously decadent dinner party dessert if warmed and served with dairy-free ice cream.

* Preheat the oven to 180°C/160°C fan/Gas 4. Grease and line the baking tin with baking parchment, leaving a couple of centimetres (about 1 inch) over at the ends to help lift the brownies out of the pan when baked.

* Melt the chocolate, dairy-free spread and soya cream together in a heatproof bowl. You can either do this over a simmering pan of water on the hob, making sure the bottom of the bowl does not touch the water, or microwave on a high setting for about 1½ minutes. Stir to make sure the ingredients have melted together.

* Place the eggs into a mixing bowl and, using a hand-held electric mixer, whisk until frothy. Add the sugar and kirsch and whisk until thick and mousselike. Add the melted chocolate mixture, whisking until combined.

* Sift the flour and xanthan gum into the mixture and fold in with a large metal spoon until combined, then stir in the 100g (3½oz of chocolate drops or chopped chocolate.

* Spoon the mixture into your brownie pan, spreading evenly and levelling the surface. Drop the cherries gently onto the surface.

* Bake in the oven for 35 minutes or until a metal skewer inserted in the middle of the brownies comes out just clean. Remove from the oven and leave to cool in the pan for a minimum of 30 minutes.

* Once cooled, remove the brownies from the tin, peel off the baking parchment and cut into pieces.

tip: If they aren't eaten straightaway, these brownies will keep for four days if stored in an airtight container. You could also freeze them for use at a later date.

Millionaire's shortbread

makes: 16 squares
preparation: 45 minutes
baking: 25 minutes
cooling: 1 hour
freeze: Yes

for the shortbread
115g (4oz) dairy-free spread
175g (6oz) wheat- and
    gluten-free plain flour
1 tsp xanthan gum
55g (2oz) caster sugar

for the caramel
125g (4½oz) dairy-free spread
125g (4½oz) caster sugar
400g (14oz) Dairy-free
    Condensed Milk
    (see page 167)
60g (2¼oz) runny honey

for the chocolate topping
100g (3½oz) good-quality
    (60% cocoa) dark dairy-
    free chocolate
100g (3½oz) dairy-free
    milk chocolate
100g (3½oz) dairy-free
    white chocolate

equipment
18cm x 27cm (7 x 10½ inch)
    shallow baking tin

tip: If you like dark
chocolate, omit the milk
chocolate and use 200g
(7oz) dark chocolate instead.

I can remember making Millionaire's Shortbread in a domestic science lesson at school years ago. On the way home, all my friends asked to try it – by the time I got home, I had two pieces left. Years later, this dairy-free version goes just as quickly!

* Preheat the oven to 180°C/160°C fan/Gas 4. Grease and line the baking tin, leaving enough lining paper hanging over the edge so you can lift the shortbread easily out of the tin.

* Place the shortbread ingredients in a food processor and blitz until they are all combined. Press firmly and evenly into the baking tin, right into the corners. Prick lightly all over with a fork.

* Bake for 20 to 25 minutes or until golden brown. Remove from the oven and leave to cool in the baking tin.

* Whilst the shortbread is cooling, make the caramel. Place the dairy-free spread into a medium-sized heavy-based saucepan and gently heat.

* Add the sugar, dairy-free condensed milk and honey, turn up to a medium heat and bring to the boil, stirring continuously. This will take about 10 minutes. Simmer and continue to stir for another 5 to 10 minutes until the mixture thickens and turns a nice caramel colour.

* Pour the caramel evenly over the cooled shortbread base. Place in the fridge to cool and firm.

* Once the caramel is firm, melt the dark and milk chocolate together in a heatproof bowl over a saucepan of simmering water, making sure the bottom of the bowl doesn't touch the water. Stir until melted and smooth.

* Pour the melted chocolate over the caramel and leave to set. Don't put it in the fridge, or the chocolate will become too hard to cut.

* In another bowl, melt the dairy-free white chocolate over a saucepan of boiling water taken off the heat. Stir continuously until melted and smooth. Drizzle the melted white chocolate over the shortbread. Leave to set.

* Once the chocolate has set, cut into squares. Although the caramel is quite firm, it will begin to soften in warm weather and go really gooey. You might prefer to store the shortbreads in an airtight container in the fridge for up to five days – that's if they last that long!

Carrot bars

makes: **16 squares**
preparation: **20 minutes**
baking: **40 minutes**
cooling: **25 minutes**
freeze: **Yes**

175g (6oz) dairy-free spread
85g (3oz) dark brown sugar
Grated zest of 1 orange
2 large eggs, beaten
55g (2oz) wheat- and
   gluten-free plain flour
1 tsp xanthan gum
1 tsp gluten-free
   baking powder
2 tsp ground mixed spice
115g (4oz) ground almonds
115g (4oz) carrots,
   coarsely grated
85g (3oz) sultanas
85g (3oz) dried apricots,
   finely chopped
55g (2oz) walnuts/pecans/
   hazelnuts, finely chopped
1 tbsp flaked almonds

equipment
18cm x 27cm (7 x 10½ inch)
   shallow baking tin

Sometimes the simplest recipes are the best. These carrot bars are so easy to make, yet they are packed with flavour and healthy ingredients and make extremely popular lunchbox treats.

* Preheat the oven to 180°C/160°C fan/Gas 4. Grease and line the baking tin, leaving enough lining paper hanging over the edge so you can lift the carrot bars out easily.

* In a large mixing bowl, use a hand-held electric mixer on a high setting to cream the dairy-free spread, sugar and grated orange zest together for about 3 minutes until light and fluffy.

* Gradually add the eggs on a medium speed setting, mixing well between each addition. Don't worry if it curdles slightly; just turn up the mixer speed to high for a few seconds and the mixture will become smooth again.

* Fold in the sifted flour, xanthan gum, baking powder, mixed spice, ground almonds, grated carrot, sultanas, chopped apricots and nuts using a large metal spoon so you don't knock the air out.

* Spoon the mixture into the lined baking tin, making sure it is evenly distributed, and level with the back of a metal spoon. Sprinkle the flaked almonds evenly over the surface.

* Bake in the oven for 35 to 40 minutes or until the cake is risen, the nuts are golden and a metal skewer inserted into the middle comes out clean.

* Remove from the oven and leave to cool in the tin for 5 minutes, then lift out of the tin, removing the baking parchment, and transfer to a metal cooling rack.

* Once cooled, cut into bars. Store in an airtight container for up to five days.

Panforte

serves: 10 to 12
preparation: 25 minutes
baking: 35 minutes
cooling: 1 hour 10 minutes
freeze: Yes, but keeps for
    several months

115g (4oz) hazelnuts
115g (4oz) almonds
125g (4½oz) candied
    mixed peel, chopped
100g (3½oz) candied
    pineapple, chopped
Finely grated zest of
    1 lemon
75g (2¾oz) wheat- and
    gluten-free plain flour
1 tsp ground cinnamon
¼ tsp ground coriander
¼ tsp ground cloves
¼ tsp grated nutmeg
Pinch of white pepper
150g (5½oz) caster sugar
4 tbsp runny honey
50g (2oz) dairy-free spread
Icing sugar, to dust

equipment
20cm (8 inch) springform
    sandwich tin and
    sugar thermometer

If, like my husband, you love nuts, then you will adore this Italian Christmas cake. Traditionally the cake tin was lined with communion paper to prevent it from sticking, but now we have the choice of using baking parchment or rice paper, which is edible, so doesn't need to be removed.

* Preheat the oven to 150°C/130°C fan/Gas 2. Grease and line the base and sides of the tin with either baking parchment or rice paper.

* Toast all your nuts by spreading them out on a baking sheet and placing in the oven for 7 to 8 minutes. Once toasted, put to one side to cool.

* Place the cooled nuts in a large mixing bowl with the mixed peel, pineapple, lemon zest, flour and spices. Toss them together so the nuts and fruit are covered in a light coating of flour and spices.

* Put the sugar, honey and dairy-free spread in a medium-sized saucepan over a gentle heat so they melt together.

* Using a sugar thermometer, cook the syrup until it reaches 118°C (245°F).

* Once the syrup has reached the required temperature, pour it into the nut mixture and mix well. You will need to work fast because the syrup firms up really quickly.

* Spoon the mixture into the prepared tin and quickly smooth the surface.

* Bake in the oven for 35 minutes or until the surface has fine blisters. Remove from the oven and leave to cool for 10 minutes.

* Whilst the cake is still warm, remove the sides of the cake tin, then carefully remove the baking parchment if you are not using rice paper and cool on a metal cooling rack.

* Dust heavily with icing sugar and store completely cooled and wrapped in clingfilm in an airtight container kept in a cool place. If wrapped well, Panforte will keep for several months.

tip: A less traditional form of Panforte, but nevertheless delicious, is Chocolate Panforte. Add 1 tablespoon cocoa powder to the flour and spice mixture and melt 90g (3oz) good-quality (60% cocoa) dark dairy-free chocolate and add to the nuts with the honey and sugar syrup. Bake as above.

Gooey chocolate
sponge traybake

serves: **20 squares**
preparation: **20 minutes**
baking: **40 minutes**
cooling: **1 hour**
freeze: **No**

for the sponge
75g (2¾oz) cocoa powder
¾ tsp bicarbonate of soda
375g (13oz) light
   muscovado sugar
180ml (6fl oz) vegetable oil
4 large eggs, beaten
200g (7oz) wheat- and gluten-
   free self-raising flour
1 tsp xanthan gum
Dairy-, wheat- and gluten-
   free hundreds and
   thousands, for decoration

for the chocolate frosting
75g (2¾oz) good-quality
   (60% cocoa) dark dairy-
   free chocolate
75g (2¾oz) dairy-free
   milk chocolate
3 tbsp soya/rice/almond milk

equipment
20cm x 30cm (8 x 12 inch)
   shallow baking tin

Another wonderfully simple yet totally delicious traybake that is a hit with everyone, especially children. It looks fab sprinkled with hundreds and thousands.

* Preheat the oven to 180°C/160°C fan/Gas 4. Grease and line the baking tin, leaving enough lining paper hanging over the edge so you can lift out the chocolate sponge easily.

* In a heatproof jug, mix the cocoa powder and bicarbonate of soda with 200ml (7fl oz) of boiling water, then put to one side to cool.

* In a large mixing bowl, use a large balloon whisk to beat the sugar, oil and eggs together. Gradually add the cocoa mixture and whisk until combined.

* Fold in the sifted flour and xanthan gum with a large metal spoon until just combined.

* Spoon the mixture into the lined baking tin, making sure it is evenly distributed, and level with the back of a metal spoon.

* Bake in the oven for 30 to 40 minutes or until the sponge is well risen and a metal skewer inserted into the middle comes out clean.

* Remove from the oven and leave to cool in the tin for 5 minutes, then lift out of the tin, removing the baking parchment, and transfer to a metal cooling rack.

* To make the frosting, gently melt the chocolate and milk in a heatproof bowl set over a saucepan of simmering water, without letting the bottom of the bowl touch the water. Stir the mixture until melted and smooth.

* Spoon the melted chocolate evenly over the traybake using a palette knife or the back of a spoon. Don't worry if it dribbles down the sides; it adds to the character of the traybake.

* Decorate with the dairy-, wheat- and gluten-free hundreds and thousands and leave to set before cutting into squares. Store in an airtight container for up to five days.

Zesty lemon squares

makes: 20 squares
preparation: 20 minutes
baking: 45 minutes
cooling: 1 hour
freeze: Yes

for the square mixture
125g (4½oz) dairy-free spread
75g (2¾oz) caster sugar
150g (5½oz) wheat- and
    gluten-free plain flour
1 tsp xanthan gum
Icing sugar, to dust

for the lemon filling
250g (9oz) caster sugar
4 large eggs, at room
    temperature and
    lightly beaten
3 tbsp lemon juice
1 tsp finely grated lemon zest
30g (1oz) wheat- and
    gluten-free plain flour
½ tsp gluten-free
    baking powder

equipment
20cm x 30cm (8 x 12 inch)
    shallow baking tin

When I asked Charlie what he thought of this traybake, it got the double thumbs-up and, in between mouthfuls, he told me it was 'Yummy, yummy, yummy,' which I took to mean he liked it!

* Preheat the oven to 180°C/160°C fan/Gas 4. Grease and line the baking tin, leaving enough lining paper hanging over the edge so you can lift out the lemon squares easily.

* In a large mixing bowl, use a hand-held electric mixer on a high setting to cream the dairy-free spread and sugar together for about 3 minutes until light and fluffy.

* Fold the sifted flour and xanthan gum in gently using a large metal spoon. Press evenly into the baking tin, making sure you reach into the corners.

* Bake in the oven for 20 minutes or until golden and firm to the touch. Leave to cool.

* To make the filling, in a large mixing bowl use a hand-held mixer on a high speed setting to cream the sugar and eggs together for about 2 minutes until light and fluffy.

* Stir in the lemon juice and zest. Sift the flour and baking powder into the mixture and, using a large balloon whisk, gradually beat until combined.

* Pour over the cooked base and bake in the oven for 25 minutes or until just firm. The filling needs to remain delicately pale. If it gets too brown, it will become crispy and difficult to cut (though it will still taste delicious).

* Remove from the oven and leave to cool in the tin. Once cool, remove from the tin, carefully remove the baking parchment and cut into squares. Store in an airtight container for up to five days.

Passion fruit
& lemon slice

makes: **16 squares**
preparation: **30 minutes**
baking: **40 minutes**
cooling: **30minutes**
freeze: **Yes**

for the base
120g (4½oz) dairy-free spread
60g (2¼oz) sifted icing sugar
½ tsp vanilla extract
185g (6½oz) wheat- and
   gluten-free plain flour
1 tsp xanthan gum
1 tsp grated lemon zest
Icing sugar, for dusting

for the filling
90g (3oz) wheat- and
   gluten-free plain flour
1 tsp xanthan gum
½ tsp gluten-free
   baking powder
65g (2½oz) desiccated
   coconut
3 large eggs, beaten and at
   room temperature
225g (8oz) caster sugar
170g (6oz) passion fruit pulp
   (approx. 7 passion fruit)
2 tbsp lemon juice
1 tsp grated lemon zest

equipment
18 x 27cm (7 x 10½ inch)
   shallow baking tin

I just love these mouthwateringly good slices. They smell and taste divine, which means I never have any left for the next day!

* Preheat the oven to 180°C/160°C fan/Gas 4. Grease and line the baking tin with baking parchment, leaving a couple of centimetres over at the ends to help lift the slice out of the pan when baked.

* To make the pastry base, use a hand-held electric mixer on a high setting to cream the dairy-free spread, icing sugar and vanilla extract together for about 3 minutes until light and fluffy.

* Fold in the flour, xanthan gum and lemon zest with a large metal spoon until you form a soft ball of dough. Using your fingers, press the soft dough evenly into the baking tin.

* Bake for 15 to 20 minutes or until lightly golden.

* Whilst the pastry base is baking, you can make the filling. Sift the flour, xanthan gum and baking powder together in a big mixing bowl, then add the coconut.

* In another bowl, lightly beat the eggs and sugar together before adding the passion fruit pulp, lemon juice and lemon zest. Fold in the flour mixture with a large metal spoon until combined.

* Remove the pastry base from the oven. Immediately spoon the passion fruit mixture evenly over the pastry base and bake in the oven for another 20 minutes or until firm to the touch.

* Remove the baked slice from the oven and leave to cool in the tin. Once cooled, dust with icing sugar and cut into slices. Store in an airtight container for up to five days.

tip: You need to persevere with folding the flour into the icing sugar and dairy-free spread mixture. It will eventually form a nice moist dough.

Salted caramel brownies

makes: 12 or 16 squares
preparation: 50 minutes
baking: 35 minutes
cooling: 1 hour 20 minutes
freeze: Yes

for the base mixture
140g (5oz) good-quality
   (60% cocoa) dark dairy-
   free chocolate
55g (2oz) dairy-free
   milk chocolate
115g (4oz) dairy-free spread
3 large eggs, beaten
280g (10oz) golden
   granulated sugar
2 tsp vanilla extract
145g (5oz) wheat- and
   gluten-free plain flour
1 tsp xanthan gum
½ tsp salt
3 tbsp cocoa powder
Fine sea salt, for decoration

for the caramel base
475g (1lb 1oz) caster sugar
1 tbsp golden syrup
175ml (6fl oz) soya
   double cream
1 tsp sea salt

equipment
18cm x 27cm (7 x 10½ inch)
   shallow baking tin and a
   sugar thermometer

The idea of salt in cakes and desserts may seem a little strange, but caramel is a flavour that really benefits from it, intensifying the flavour. I can clearly remember the first time I made this recipe. The anticipation waiting for the brownies to cool enough to eat was so strong I had to do a little housework to distract myself – and then that first bite, sheer heaven. To make caramel, you do need a sugar thermometer. They aren't expensive and will be a great investment, especially if you really like caramel and toffee!

* Preheat the oven to 180°C/160°C fan/Gas 4. Grease and line the baking tin, leaving enough lining paper hanging over the edge so you can lift out the brownies easily.

* First, make the caramel sauce. Place the sugar, 125ml (4fl oz) water and the golden syrup in a heavy-based saucepan and heat over a high heat, stirring occasionally, until the syrup becomes clear.

* Clip a sugar thermometer to the side of the saucepan and stop stirring. Cook the syrup until it comes to the boil. Continue to boil, gently swirling the saucepan occasionally, until the syrup just reaches 180°C (356°F) and caramelizes. Keep an eye on the syrup because if the caramel burns, you won't be able to use it.

* Remove from the heat and very slowly spoon in the soya cream (be careful because it will spatter). Stir with a wooden spoon until the cream has been combined and is nice and smooth. Stir in the sea salt. Cover and put to one side. If the caramel begins to harden at any time, gently reheat it until it is pourable again.

* Now, make the brownies. Melt the chocolates and dairy-free spread together in a heatproof bowl. You can either do this over a simmering pan of water on the stove, making sure the bottom of the bowl does not touch the water, or, like me, use the microwave on a high setting for about 1½ minutes. Stir to make sure the ingredients have melted together.

* Using a hand-held electric mixer on a high speed setting, beat the eggs, sugar and vanilla together for 30 seconds.

recipe continues...

tip: You will have lots of caramel sauce left, but it can be stored in the fridge for up to two weeks, so why not use the excuse to treat yourself to indulgent caramel-coated puddings and drizzled ice creams. You will probably need to gently warm the caramel when you take it out of the fridge.

* Gradually add the melted chocolate and dairy-free spread using a slow mixer speed until the mixture is well combined.

* Gently fold in the sifted flour, xanthan gum, salt and cocoa powder through the creamy mixture, using long folding motions (you don't want to beat the air out).

* Spoon half the mixture into the lined baking tin, making sure it is evenly distributed, and level with the back of a metal spoon.

* Spoon six dessert spoons of caramel on top of the mixture, being careful not to put them too close to the edge of the pan, as the caramel will ooze out and stick to the baking parchment.

* Carefully spoon the remaining half of the brownie mixture over the top of the caramel, making sure it is evenly distributed and level.

* Spoon another six dessert spoons of caramel on the top, again being careful not to get them too close to the edge of the pan.

* Using a round-bladed knife, very carefully swirl the caramel through the brownie mixture. Don't swirl too much, as we don't want the caramel to be mixed into the chocolate mixture, we just want a nice swirly pattern.

* Bake in the oven for 35 minutes. You might think they don't look cooked and be tempted to leave them in for longer, but don't – brownies continue to cook and firm up as they cool.

* Leave the brownies to cool in the tin for 1 hour, if you can last that long! They will be easier to cut the longer you leave them. Sprinkle the cooked brownies with a few flakes of sea salt.

* Remove the brownies from the tin, peel off the baking parchment, and leave to finish cooling on a metal cooling rack. Once cold, cut into squares using a large plastic knife if you have one. If you don't, use a large sharp knife heated in hot water in between slices. This will stop you getting into a lovely gooey mess.

Boozy apricot
macaroon traybake

makes: **20 squares**
preparation: **40 minutes**
baking: **55 minutes**
cooling: **1 hour**
freeze: **Yes**

for the pastry base
100g (3½oz) dairy-free spread
80g (3oz) caster sugar
1 large egg, beaten
**185g (6½oz) wheat- and
   gluten-free plain flour**
1 tsp xanthan gum
**½ tsp gluten-free
   baking powder**

for the apricot filling
**250g (9oz) dried apricots,
   chopped**
1 tbsp Grand Marnier
2 tbsp caster sugar

ingredients continue...

For some reason I think of this recipe as being autumnal. I don't know why – perhaps it's the touch of alcohol or the dried apricots – but whatever the reason, I particularly enjoy baking it when the children start back to school in September! (See picture on page 114.)

* Preheat the oven to 180°C/160°C fan/Gas 4. Grease and line the baking tin with baking parchment, leaving a couple of centimetres (about 1 inch) over at the ends to help lift the slice out of the pan when baked.

* Combine the apricots, Grand Marnier, sugar and 125ml (4fl oz) of boiling water and put the apricots to one side to soak for 30 minutes.

* To make the pastry base, use a hand-held electric mixer on a high setting to cream the dairy-free spread and sugar together for about 3 minutes until light and fluffy.

* Gradually add the beaten egg on a medium speed setting until combined. Don't worry if the mixture curdles slightly; just turn the mixer setting up to high for a couple of seconds and the mixture will become smooth again.

* Fold in the flour, xanthan gum and baking powder with a large metal spoon until you form a soft ball of dough. Using your fingers, press the soft dough evenly into the baking tin.

* Bake for 25 to 30 minutes or until lightly golden.

* Whilst the pastry base is baking, you can finish making the filling. Purée the apricot mixture in a food processor and put to one side.

* Remove the pastry base from the oven and leave to cool for 5 minutes in the tin. Spoon the apricot purée over the cooled pastry base.

* To make the topping, use a hand-held electric mixer on a high setting to cream the dairy-free spread, vanilla extract and sugar together for about 3 minutes until light and fluffy.

recipe continues...

for the macaroon topping
100g (3½oz) dairy-free spread

1 tsp vanilla extract

80g (3oz) caster sugar

2 large eggs, beaten

280g (10oz) desiccated
   coconut

40g (1½oz) wheat- and
   gluten-free plain flour

½ tsp xanthan gum

½ tsp gluten-free
   baking powder

equipment

20cm x 30cm (8 x 12 inch)
   shallow baking tin

* Gradually add the beaten eggs on a medium speed setting until combined. Don't worry if the mixture curdles slightly, just turn the mixer setting up to high for a couple of seconds and the mixture will become smooth again.

* Fold in the coconut, flour, xanthan gum and baking powder with a large metal spoon until you form a soft ball of dough. Spoon evenly onto the apricot purée.

* Bake in the oven for 20 to 25 minutes or until golden in colour. Remove from the oven and leave to cool in the tin for 30 minutes. Remove from the tin and finish cooling on a metal cooling rack.

* Once cool, cut into squares. Store in an airtight container for up to three days.

tip: If you don't have any Grand Marnier or you don't like it, you can replace it with 2 tablespoons fresh orange juice.

Chocolate
peanut butter squares

serves: 12 or 16 squares
preparation: 20 minutes
baking: 30 minutes
cooling: 1½ hours
freeze: Yes

200g (7oz) good-quality
   (60% cocoa) dark dairy-
   free chocolate
225g (8oz) soft light
   brown sugar
125g (4½oz) dairy-free spread
65g (2¼oz) crunchy
   peanut butter
2 large eggs, beaten
125g (4½oz) wheat- and
   gluten-free plain flour
30g (1oz) wheat- and gluten-
   free self-raising flour
1 tsp xanthan gum
80g (3oz) unsalted roasted
   peanuts, roughly chopped
100g (3½oz) good-quality
   (60% cocoa) dark dairy-
   free chocolate, chips
   or roughly chopped,
   for decoration

equipment
18cm x 27cm (7 x 10½inch)
   shallow baking tin

Chocolate and peanut butter is such an American combination and one that works so well. I first tried these chocolate squares on holiday in Chicago and have spent years trying to recapture that delicious flavour. I have finally managed it.

* Preheat the oven to 170°C/150°C fan/Gas 3. Grease and line the baking tin, leaving enough lining paper hanging over the edge so you can lift the squares easily out of the tin.

* Melt the 200g (7oz) chocolate in a heatproof bowl set over a saucepan of simmering water, making sure the bottom of the bowl does not touch the water. Stir occasionally until the chocolate has completely melted. Remove from the heat and leave to cool.

* Using a hand-held electric mixer on a high speed setting, beat the sugar, dairy-free spread and peanut butter together until the mixture becomes nice and thick.

* Gradually add the eggs on a medium speed setting, mixing well between each addition. Gently stir in the melted chocolate, sifted flours, xanthan gum and the chopped peanuts. The mixture will become quite thick and sticky.

* Spoon the mixture into the lined baking tin, making sure it is evenly distributed, and level with the back of a metal spoon. Press the chocolate chips or chopped chocolate into the surface.

* Bake in the preheated oven for 30 minutes or until a metal skewer inserted into the middle comes out clean (try not to spear a chunk of chocolate!).

* Leave the chocolate and peanut butter squares to cool in the tin for 1 hour. They will be easier to cut the longer you leave them.

* Remove the squares from the tin, peel off the baking parchment and leave to finish cooling on a metal cooling rack. Once cold, cut into squares using a large plastic knife if you have one. If you don't, use a large sharp knife, heated in hot water between slices. This will stop you getting into a lovely gooey mess. Store in an airtight container for up to seven days.

Cupcakes
&
Muffins

Chocolate cupcakes

makes: 18 muffin-sized
  cupcakes
preparation: 25 minutes
baking: 25 minutes
cooling: 35 minutes
freeze: Yes

for the cupcake mixture
240ml (8fl oz) soya milk
1 tbsp lemon juice
375g (13oz) wheat- and
  gluten-free self-raising
  flour, less 3 tbsp
3 tbsp cocoa powder
2 tsp xanthan gum
1 tsp bicarbonate of soda
1 tsp salt
290g (10oz) caster sugar
2 large eggs
1 tsp vanilla extract
275ml (9¾fl oz) vegetable oil
1 tsp distilled vinegar
Grated chocolate,
  for decoration
Edible glitter, for decoration
1 x Chocolate Frosting
  (see page 168)

equipment
12- and 6-hole muffin tins

tip: If you have a lot of
frosting left over, don't worry;
just place it in a freezer bag
and freeze for up to 1 month.

I often bake a batch of these to take to Charlie's school fête and it's great to see the children's eyes grow wide with wonder when they see them. Wonderfully light and fluffy sponge, topped with real chocolate frosting and decorated with a dusting of grated chocolate and a sprinkle of edible glitter – they are always a hit!

* Preheat the oven to 180°C/160°C fan/Gas 4. Line the tins with muffin cases.

* Heat the soya milk in a small heavy-based saucepan over a gentle heat until warm or heat in the microwave on high for 40 seconds. Take the milk off the heat, add the lemon juice and stir until the milk begins to thicken and look curdled, then put to one side. You now have dairy-free buttermilk.

* Mix the flour, cocoa powder, xanthan gum, bicarbonate of soda, salt and sugar in a large bowl, then sift into another large bowl and put to one side.

* In a large mixing bowl and using a balloon whisk, beat together the eggs, vanilla extract, vegetable oil, buttermilk and distilled vinegar.

* Slowly add the flour mixture in three stages to the egg and oil mixture, gently stirring with the balloon whisk. Be careful not to overmix.

* Divide the mixture evenly among the muffin cases, filling each three-quarters full. I use a level ice-cream scoop of mixture, which ensures an equal amount in each case. The mixture will be quite firm, so level with the back of a teaspoon.

* Bake in the middle of the oven for 20 minutes or until the cakes are well risen and the sponge springs back when touched. If necessary, rotate the tins and finish baking for a further 2 minutes.

* Remove from the oven and leave to cool in the tins for 5 minutes before transferring to a metal cooling rack.

* Pipe the frosting onto the cooled cupcakes and decorate with the grated chocolate and/or edible glitter. If you don't use the frosting immediately, it will firm up, so stir in a little more soya milk until you have the right consistency.

Red velvet cupcakes

makes: 18 cupcakes
preparation: 20 minutes
baking: 25 minutes
cooling: 35 minutes
freeze: You can freeze the
    cakes before icing them

225ml (8fl oz) soya milk
1 tbsp lemon juice
375g (13oz) wheat-
    and gluten-free
    self-raising flour
2 tsp xanthan gum
1 tsp bicarbonate of soda
1 tsp cocoa powder
1 tsp salt
290g (10oz) caster sugar
2 large eggs
1 tsp vanilla extract
275ml (9¾fl oz) vegetable oil
25g (1oz) red food colouring
1 tsp distilled vinegar
2 x Dairy-free Cream
    (see page 170)

equipment
12- and 6-hole muffin tins

I am frequently asked by my customers, 'What is a red velvet cake?' Well, apart from being the best-selling cupcake in America, and quite possibly now in the UK too, these little cakes were what really made me feel I was missing out. Reputably, the cakes date back to the 1900s, when it was discovered that cocoa powder reacted with the acid in buttermilk to give the sponge its reddish brown appearance. These days we don't worry about 'reactions' and use a dose of good old food colouring to achieve the desired red colour. And whilst we now expect the cakes to be topped with cream cheese frosting, they were originally topped with a more traditional flour-based cream. This, of course, suits me perfectly, and I have to say it suits a lot of my customers as well. The dairy-free cream frosting is totally delicious and not as sweet as cream cheese frosting, so although you might think it strange to use flour in a frosting, I can assure you it works brilliantly.

* Preheat the oven to 180°C/160°C fan/Gas 4. Line the tins with muffin cases.

* Heat the soya milk in a small heavy-based saucepan over a gentle heat until warm or heat in a microwave on high for 40 seconds. Take the milk off the heat, add the lemon juice and stir until the milk begins to thicken and look curdled, then put to one side. You now have dairy-free buttermilk.

* Mix the flour, xanthan gum, bicarbonate of soda, cocoa powder, salt and sugar in a large bowl, then sift into another large bowl and put to one side.

* In a large mixing bowl and using a balloon whisk, beat together the eggs, vanilla extract, vegetable oil, buttermilk, red food colouring and distilled vinegar.

recipe continues...

tip: To get the right depth of colour for a red velvet, use either Dr. Oetker or Silver Spoon Red Colouring, not the Natural Red, which is too dark. I have tried making the dairy-free cream frosting with rice and almond milk, but it just doesn't work as well. Soya milk is much thicker and creamier, like cow's milk, so it works well.

* Slowly add the flour mixture in three stages to the egg and oil mixture, gently stirring with the balloon whisk. Be careful not to overmix.

* Divide the mixture evenly among the muffin cases, filling each three-quarters full. I use a level ice-cream scoop of mixture, which ensures an equal amount in each case.

* Bake in the middle of the oven for 20 minutes or until the cakes are well risen and the sponge springs back when touched. If necessary, rotate the tins and finish baking for a further 2 minutes.

* Remove from the oven and leave to cool in the tins for 5 minutes before transferring to a metal cooling rack.

* Pipe the dairy-free cream frosting onto the cooled cupcakes and decorate as required.

Lemon butterfly cakes

makes: 12 muffin-sized
    cupcakes
preparation: 25 minutes
baking: 30 minutes
cooling: 35 minutes
freeze: Yes

200g (7oz) dairy-free spread
200g (7oz) caster sugar
Grated zest of 1 lemon
4 large eggs, beaten
200g (7oz) wheat-
    and gluten-free
    self-raising flour
2 tsp xanthan gum
1 x Lemon Curd
    (see page 168)
Icing sugar, for decoration

equipment
12-hole muffin tin

tip: To make orange
butterfly cakes, simply
exchange the lemon zest
for orange zest. To make
orange curd, replace the
lemon juice and zest with
orange juice and zest for
a lovely subtle curd.

Butterfly cakes are often associated with children's parties and quite rightly so – children love them. These butterfly cakes, however, are quite grown up and filled with deliciously tangy lemon curd that positively melts in the mouth.

* Preheat the oven to 180°C/160°C fan/Gas 4. Line the tin with muffin cases.

* In a large mixing bowl, use a hand-held mixer on a high speed setting to cream together the dairy-free spread, sugar and lemon zest for about 3 minutes until light and fluffy.

* Gradually add the beaten eggs on a medium speed setting, mixing well between each addition. Don't worry if the mixture curdles slightly; just turn the mixer setting up to high for a couple of seconds and the mixture will become smooth again.

* Fold in the sifted flour and xanthan gum using a large metal spoon so you don't knock the air out.

* Divide the mixture evenly among the muffin cases, filling each three-quarters full. I use a level ice cream scoop of mixture, which ensures an equal amount in each case. The mixture is quite firm, so level with the back of a teaspoon.

* Bake in the middle of the oven for 20 to 25 minutes or until the cakes are well risen, golden and the sponge springs back when touched. If necessary, rotate the tin and finish baking for a further 2 minutes.

* Remove from the oven and leave to cool in the tins for 5 minutes before transferring to a metal cooling rack.

* Once the cakes have cooled and using a small, sharp knife, cut a small cone shape out of the centre of each cake. Cut the cones in half to make the wings.

* Either pipe or spoon the chilled lemon curd into the hollowed-out cone shape, then place the two cone halves on top. Dust the cakes with icing sugar to finish.

Mega chocolate muffins

makes: 12 muffin-sized
   cakes
preparation: 25 minutes
baking: 25 minutes
cooling: 35 minutes
freeze: You can freeze the
   muffins before icing them

for the cupcake mixture
175g (6oz) good-quality
   (60% cocoa) dark
   dairy-free chocolate
175g (6oz) dairy-free spread
175g (6oz) caster sugar
4 large eggs, beaten
½ tsp vanilla extract
175g (6oz) wheat-
   and gluten-free
   self-raising flour
1 tsp gluten-free
   baking powder
1 tsp xanthan gum
Small bar of cold dark
   dairy-free chocolate,
   for grating (optional)

for the chocolate ganache
115g (4oz) good-quality
   (60% cocoa) dark dairy-
   free chocolate
125ml (4fl oz) soya
   double cream

equipment
12-hole muffin tin

These muffins really are the business. They are wonderfully light and chocolaty with a crispy top. To enjoy your muffins at their best, you really should eat them the day they are baked, but these taste good several days later if you store them in an airtight container.

* Preheat the oven to 200°C/180°C fan/Gas 6. Line the tins with muffin cases.

* To make the muffins, melt the chocolate and dairy-free spread in a heatproof bowl over a small saucepan of simmering water, making sure the bottom of the bowl doesn't touch the water. Stir until smooth and melted.

* Remove the chocolate from the heat and stir in the sugar. Leave to cool slightly.

* Beat in the eggs and vanilla extract using a large balloon whisk. Gently fold in the sifted flour, baking powder and xanthan gum using a large metal spoon.

* Divide the mixture evenly among the muffin cases. I use a level ice-cream scoop of mixture, which ensures an equal amount in each case.

* Bake for 20 to 25 minutes or until well risen and springy to the touch. Remove from the oven and leave to cool in the tins for 5 minutes, then turn out onto a metal cooling rack.

* Whilst the muffins are cooling, you can make the ganache. Melt the chocolate and cream in a heatproof bowl over a saucepan of simmering water, making sure the bottom of the bowl doesn't touch the water. Stir occasionally until melted. Remove the bowl from the heat and stir the ganache until smooth. Using a hand-held electric mixer on a high speed setting, beat the ganache until it becomes paler and lighter.

* Using a round-bladed knife, spread the cooled ganache over the top of the muffins. Dust with finely grated dark chocolate if you wish.

tip: You will get a much firmer ganache if you use a really good-quality dark chocolate with a minimum of 60% cocoa content.

Banana, cranberry & pecan muffins

makes: **12 muffin-sized cakes**
preparation: **25 minutes**
baking: **25 minutes**
cooling: **35 minutes**
freeze: **yes**

80g (3oz) dairy-free spread
225g (8oz) wheat- and gluten-free self-raising flour
1 tsp gluten-free baking powder
1 tsp xanthan gum
½ tsp bicarbonate of soda
150g (5½oz) golden caster sugar
2 ripe bananas, mashed
2 large eggs, beaten
4 tbsp dairy-free sour cream
½ tsp vanilla extract
50g (2oz) dried cranberries
50g (2oz) pecan nuts, chopped

equipment
12-hole muffin tin

These moreish muffins make a great lunchbox or picnic treat. The bananas help to keep them moist, so you can happily store them for a few days in an airtight container until needed.

* Preheat the oven to 200°C/180°C fan/Gas 6. Line the tin with muffin cases.
* Melt the dairy-free spread in a small heavy-based saucepan over a gentle heat. Once melted, remove from the heat and leave to cool.
* Sift the flour, baking powder, xanthan gum and bicarbonate of soda into a large mixing bowl. Stir in the sugar.
* Make a well in the middle of the dry ingredients and add the mashed bananas, beaten eggs, sour cream, vanilla extract, melted dairy-free spread, dried cranberries and chopped pecan nuts.
* Using a large metal spoon, fold the ingredients until just mixed. Don't overmix, otherwise the muffins will have a rubbery texture.
* Divide the mixture evenly among the cases. I use a level ice-cream scoop of mixture, which ensures an equal amount in each case. Using the back of a teaspoon, level the mixture out.
* Bake for 20 to 25 minutes until the muffins have risen and are just firm to the touch. Remove from the oven and leave to cool in the tins for 5 minutes. Transfer to a metal cooling rack.

tip: I love the chewy texture of dried cranberries, but you can use any other dried fruit. You could also swap the pecans for walnuts if you prefer.

Black Forest cupcakes

makes: 12 cupcakes
preparation: 1 hour
baking: 25 minutes
cooling: 3 hours
freeze: You can freeze the
    cupcakes before filling
    them

for the cupcake mixture
225ml (8fl oz) soya milk
1 tbsp lemon juice
200g (7oz) wheat-
    and gluten-free
    self-raising flour
2 tsp xanthan gum
60g (2¼oz) cocoa powder
1 tsp bicarbonate of soda
Pinch of salt
140g (5oz) dairy-free spread
115g (4oz) granulated sugar
85g (3oz) dark brown sugar
2 large eggs, beaten
75ml (2½fl oz) dairy-free
    sour cream
2 tbsp kirsch
1 jar (net weight 470g/1lb
    1oz) pitted Morello
    cherries in syrup

ingredients continue...

These rather wonderful layered cupcakes make an impressive dinner party dessert and although at first glance they appear to be a lot of work, each stage can be prepared separately. The cupcakes can be made in advance and frozen for up to two months, while the pastry cream and chocolate ganache can be made the day before and stored in the fridge. That means all you have to do is assemble them just before serving – easy.

* Preheat the oven to 180°C/160°C fan/Gas 4. Filled and layered cupcakes work much better when baked without muffin cases, so brush the muffin tins with dairy-free spread and dust with cocoa powder, tapping out the excess.

* First, make the pastry cream. In a large bowl and using a large balloon whisk, beat the egg yolks until smooth.

* Combine the sugar, salt and cornflour in a heavy-based saucepan over a medium heat and slowly pour in the milk in a steady stream, stirring constantly. Cook until the mixture thickens and begins to bubble, which should take between 5 and 8 minutes.

* Once the mixture has thickened, slowly pour a third of the mixture into the egg yolks, whisk to combine, then slowly pour back into the saucepan. Continue to cook over the medium heat, stirring constantly, for 5 to 10 minutes until the mixture comes to a full boil. This is very important because if the mixture doesn't boil properly, the cream won't thicken. Once the mixture is thick enough to hold its shape, remove from the heat and whisk in the vanilla extract.

* Strain the mixture through a fine sieve into a heatproof bowl. Cover with clingfilm, making sure it is pressed onto the cream to prevent a skin forming. Pop into the fridge for a couple of hours to chill and firm.

* To make the cupcakes, heat the soya milk in a small heavy-based saucepan over a gentle heat until warm or heat in a microwave on high for 40 seconds. Take the milk off the heat, add the lemon juice and stir until the milk begins to thicken and look curdled, then put to one side. You now have dairy-free buttermilk.

recipe continues...

for the pastry cream
4 large egg yolks
100g (3½oz) caster sugar
Pinch of salt
30g (1oz) cornflour
425ml (15fl oz) soya milk
¾ tsp vanilla extract

for the chocolate ganache
175g (6oz) good-quality
(60% cocoa) dark dairy-
  free chocolate
140ml (5fl oz) soya
  double cream
1 tbsp golden syrup

equipment
12-hole muffin tin

....

tip: If you prefer, these layered cupcakes can be baked in muffin cases; they just won't have the nice smooth sides to them. Ensure you carefully remove them from their cases once they have cooled. If using frozen cupcakes, allow 3 to 4 hours for them to defrost at room temperature.

* Sift the flour, xanthan gum, cocoa powder, bicarbonate of soda and salt into a large mixing bowl and put to one side.

* In another large mixing bowl, use a hand-held electric mixer on a high speed setting to cream the dairy-free spread and granulated sugar together for about 3 minutes until light and fluffy.

* Add the dark brown sugar and beat until fluffy. Gradually add the eggs on a medium speed setting, mixing well between each addition. Don't worry if the mixture curdles slightly; just turn the mixer speed up to high for a few seconds and the mixture will become smooth again. Beat in the sour cream.

* Using a large metal spoon, fold in the flour mixture in three batches, alternating with the buttermilk, then mix until just combined.

* Divide the mixture evenly among the holes in the muffin tin. I use a heaped ice cream scoop of mixture, which ensures an equal amount in each hole. The mixture will be quite firm, so level with the back of a teaspoon.

* Bake in the middle of the oven for 20 minutes or until the cakes are well risen and the sponge springs back when touched. If necessary, rotate the tins and finish baking for a further 2 minutes.

* Remove from the oven and leave to cool in the tins for 5 minutes before transferring to a metal cooling rack.

* Whilst the cupcakes are cooling, make the chocolate ganache. Place the chocolate in a medium-sized heatproof mixing bowl. Heat the cream and golden syrup in a small heavy-based saucepan over a medium heat. Stir until the mixture melts.

* Pour over the chocolate and leave to stand, without stirring, for a couple of minutes. Once the chocolate has started to melt, slowly stir with a wooden spoon to combine. You want the mixture to become smooth and glossy. Put to one side.

* Once the cupcakes have cooled, use a serrated knife to gently cut the tops off the cakes and put to one side. Mix the kirsch with 50ml (2fl oz) of the cherry syrup and brush both cut sides of the cupcake with the syrup mixture.

* Cut the cherries in half and arrange on the cupcake bottom. Spoon a tablespoon of pastry cream over the top of the cherries and pop the top halves back on.

* Spoon 2 tbsp of chocolate ganache over the tops of the cakes and pop into the fridge to chill for 15 minutes before serving.

* These cupcakes are best eaten the day you bake them, but they can be stored overnight in an airtight container.

Milk chocolate
& hazelnut cupcakes

makes: **12 muffin-sized cupcakes**
preparation: **30 minutes**
baking: **25 minutes**
cooling: **35 minutes**
freeze: **Yes**

100g (3½oz) dairy-free milk chocolate
6 tbsp soya/rice/almond milk
175g (6oz) dairy-free spread
175g (6oz) soft light brown sugar
4 large eggs, beaten
1 tsp vanilla extract
150g (5½oz) wheat- and gluten-free self-raising flour
1 tsp xanthan gum
½ tsp gluten-free baking powder
100g (3½oz) ground hazelnuts
1 x Chocolate Frosting (see page 168)

equipment
12-hole muffin tin

tip: If you cannot find ground hazelnuts, you can grind whole toasted nuts in small batches – but don't overgrind, otherwise you will end up making hazelnut butter!

Using milk chocolate in these cupcakes makes them less rich and slightly sweeter, which is no bad thing. Children absolutely love them.

* Preheat the oven to 180°C/160°C fan/Gas 4. Line the tin with muffin cases.

* Melt the chocolate and milk in a heatproof bowl over a small saucepan of simmering water, making sure the bottom of the bowl doesn't touch the water. Stir until smooth and melted.

* In a large mixing bowl, use a hand-held electric mixer on a high speed setting to cream together the dairy-free spread and sugar for about 3 minutes until light and fluffy.

* Gradually add the beaten eggs and vanilla extract on a medium speed setting, mixing well between each addition. Don't worry if the mixture curdles slightly; just turn the mixer setting up to high for a couple of seconds and the mixture will become smooth again.

* Gradually add the melted chocolate and milk, mixing well until combined.

* Slowly fold in the sifted flour, xanthan gum, baking powder and ground hazelnuts using a large metal spoon so you don't knock the air out.

* Divide the mixture evenly among the muffin cases, filling each three-quarters full. I use a level ice cream scoop of mixture, which ensures an equal amount in each case. The mixture is quite firm, so level with the back of a teaspoon.

* Bake in the middle of the oven for 20 minutes or until the cakes are well risen and the sponge springs back when touched. If necessary, rotate the tin and finish baking for a further 2 minutes.

* Remove the cupcakes from the oven and leave to cool in the tins for 5 minutes before transferring to a metal cooling rack.

* When the cupcakes have cooled completely, pipe on the chocolate frosting and decorate.

* The cupcakes will keep for five days if stored in an airtight container. Do not keep in the fridge.

Orange, pistachio
& polenta cupcakes with syrup

makes: **12 muffin-sized cupcakes**
preparation: **30 minutes**
baking: **25 minutes**
cooling: **35 minutes**
freeze: **Yes**

for the cupcake mixture
100g (3½oz) pistachio
   nuts, shelled
2 large eggs
1 tsp vanilla extract
Grated zest of 1 orange
200g (7oz) dairy-free spread
160g (5½oz) caster sugar
60g (2¼oz) wheat-
   and gluten-free
   self-raising flour
1 tsp xanthan gum
185g (6½oz) coarse polenta
125ml (4fl oz) orange juice

for the orange syrup
125g (4½oz) caster sugar
60ml (2¼fl oz) orange juice

equipment
12-hole muffin tin

These cupcakes have a lovely crunchy texture. However, if you prefer, you can pour the mixture into an 18cm x 27cm (7 x 10½ inch) baking tin and make a delicious traybake. Just double the quantity of the syrup and bake for 30 minutes.

* Preheat the oven to 180°C/160°C fan/Gas 4. Line the tin with muffin cases. Toast the pistachios by spreading them out on a baking sheet and placing in the oven for 7 to 8 minutes. Remove from the oven, cool and chop finely.

* In a small bowl, lightly beat the eggs, vanilla extract and orange zest together, then put to one side.

* In a large mixing bowl, use a hand-held electric mixer on a high speed setting to cream the dairy-free spread and sugar together for about 3 minutes until light and fluffy.

* Gradually add the egg mixture on a medium speed setting, mixing well between each addition. Don't worry if the mixture curdles slightly; just turn the mixer setting up high for a couple of seconds and the mixture will become smooth again.

* Carefully fold in the flour, xanthan gum, polenta, orange juice and chopped pistachio nuts. Don't overfold – the ingredients need to be just combined. Divide the mixture evenly among the muffin cases, using an ice-cream scoop to ensure an equal amount in each case.

* Bake in the oven for 20 to 25 minutes or until the cakes are well risen, golden and spring back when touched. If necessary, rotate the tin and finish baking for a further few minutes.

* Whilst the cupcakes are in the oven, prepare the syrup. In a small heavy-based saucepan, mix the caster sugar and orange juice together, slowly bring to the boil and simmer for 1 minute.

* Remove the cupcakes from the oven and spoon 3 teaspoons of syrup over each cupcake. Leave the cakes in the tin until the syrup has soaked in. Transfer to a metal cooling rack to finish cooling.

* Store in an airtight container for up to five days, but not in the fridge.

Almond

& cherry cupcakes

makes: 12 muffin-sized
   cupcakes
preparation: 25 minutes
baking: 25 minutes
cooling: 35 minutes
freeze: Yes

for the cupcake mixture
200g (7oz) dairy-free spread
200g (7oz) caster sugar
4 large eggs, beaten
100g (3½oz) wheat-
   and gluten-free
   self-raising flour
100g (3½oz) ground almonds
1 tsp almond extract
2 tsp xanthan gum
4 tbsp raspberry jam
6 glacé cherries, halved

for the icing
Juice of 1 lemon
225 (8oz) sifted icing sugar

equipment
12-hole muffin tin and an
   apple corer

Inspiration for these delicious cupcakes came from the classic Bakewell tart. The ground almonds make a really moist sponge and the slightly chewy glacé icing on top just adds to the pleasure.

* Preheat the oven to 180°C/160°C fan/Gas 4. Line the tin with muffin cases.

* In a large mixing bowl, use a hand-held electric mixer on a high speed setting to cream together the dairy-free spread and sugar for about 3 minutes until light and fluffy.

* Gradually add the beaten eggs on a medium speed setting, mixing well between each addition. Don't worry if the mixture curdles slightly; just turn the mixer setting up to high for a couple of seconds and the mixture will become smooth again.

* Fold in the sifted flour, ground almonds, almond extract and xanthan gum using a large metal spoon so you don't knock the air out.

* Divide the mixture evenly among the muffin cases, filling each three-quarters full. I use a level ice-cream scoop of mixture, which ensures an equal amount in each case. The mixture is quite firm, so level with the back of a teaspoon.

* Bake in the middle of the oven for 20 minutes or until the cakes are well risen, golden and the sponge springs back when touched. If necessary, rotate the tin and finish baking for a further 2 minutes.

* Remove from the oven and leave to cool in the tins for 5 minutes before transferring to a metal cooling rack.

* Whilst the cupcakes are cooling, make the glacé icing. Gently warm the lemon juice in a small heavy-based saucepan over a low heat (this will help the icing to set).

* Gradually add the warmed lemon juice to the sifted icing sugar, beating together until you have a nice glossy icing. If it is a little runny, add some extra icing sugar. If it is a little too firm, add some more lemon juice.

recipe continues...

tip: If you don't have an apple corer, use a small sharp knife to cut a plug out of the sponge. Just remember not to cut right through to the bottom of the cakes.

* Place the raspberry jam in a small bowl and stir until smooth and runny. Using the apple corer, remove a plug of sponge out of the middle of each cupcake. Slice the top off each plug of sponge and put to one side.

* Pour a teaspoon of jam into each cupcake and pop the sliced sponge top back on top to seal it in. Spoon the glacé icing over the top of the cupcakes and decorate with half a glacé cherry.

* Store the cakes in an airtight container for up to five days.

Blueberry & lemon friands

makes: 12 muffin-sized cakes
preparation: 25 minutes
baking: 20 minutes
cooling: 35 minutes
freeze: Yes

200g (7oz) dairy-free spread
250g (9oz) icing sugar
50g (2oz) wheat- and
  gluten-free plain flour
1 tsp xanthan gum
175g (6oz) ground almonds
6 egg whites
Grated zest of 2 lemons
175g (6oz) blueberries
Icing sugar, for dusting

equipment
12-hole muffin tin

tip: In Australia, friands are baked in small oval tins without cases. These can be hard to find in the UK, so I use muffin tins with cases.

If you have never heard of friands, then you are in for a treat. They originate from Australia and are cousins of the French Financiers, the delicious moist egg-white cakes. Friands differ in that they use melted fat and are normally full of fruit or nuts. Once you have tried them, there is no going back. Get practising – they could just be the next cupcakes!

* Preheat the oven to 200°C/180°C fan/Gas 6. Line the tin with paper cases.

* Melt the dairy-free spread in a heavy-based saucepan over a gentle heat and set aside to cool.

* Sift the icing sugar, flour and xanthan gum into a mixing bowl. Add the almonds and mix between your fingers.

* In another bowl, whisk the egg whites until they form a light floppy foam.

* Make a well in the centre of the dry ingredients, gently pour in the egg whites and add the lemon zest. Gently stir in the melted dairy-free spread to form a soft batter.

* Divide the batter among the cases, using a jug to help with the spills. Sprinkle a handful of blueberries over each cake.

* Bake for 15 to 20 minutes or until golden brown and firm to the touch. Remove from the oven and leave to cool in the tins for 5 minutes, then turn out and cool on a metal cooling rack.

* Dust with icing sugar to serve.

Strawberry cupcakes
with meringue frosting

makes: 18 muffin-sized
   cupcakes
preparation: 40 minutes
baking: 35 minutes
cooling: 35 minutes
freeze: No

for the cupcake mixture
2 large eggs + 2 large
   egg whites
1 tsp vanilla extract
160g (5½oz) dairy-free
   spread
300g (10½oz) caster sugar
300g (10½oz) wheat-
   and gluten-free
   self-raising flour
½ tsp salt
2 tsp xanthan gum
125ml (4fl oz) soya/rice/
   almond milk
12 large strawberries,
   chopped

for the meringue frosting
1 x Seven-minute Frosting
   (see page 167)
A couple of drops of
   strawberry flavouring,
   if desired
10 strawberries, sliced,
   to decorate

equipment
6- and 12-hole muffin tins

Summer hopefully brings a glut of beautifully sweet strawberries, and what better way to use them than in these pretty cupcakes? Topped with the light and fluffy meringue frosting and decorated with slices of strawberry, they make a perfect addition to any tea party.

* Preheat the oven to 180°C/160°C fan/Gas 4. Line the tins with muffin cases.

* Blend the eggs, egg whites and vanilla together with a fork and put to one side.

* In a large mixing bowl, use a hand-held electric mixer on a high speed setting to cream together the dairy-free spread and sugar for about 3 minutes until light and fluffy.

* Gradually add the beaten eggs and vanilla extract on a medium speed setting, mixing well between each addition. Don't worry if the mixture curdles slightly; just turn the mixer setting up to high for a couple of seconds and the mixture will become smooth again.

* Fold in the sifted flour, salt and xanthan gum in two batches, alternating with the milk and using a large metal spoon so you don't knock the air out. Gently fold in the chopped strawberries.

* Divide the mixture evenly among the muffin cases, filling each three-quarters full. I use a heaped ice-cream scoop of mixture, which ensures an equal amount in each case. Level the mixture with the back of a teaspoon.

* Bake in the middle of the oven for 25 to 30 minutes or until the cakes are well risen, golden and the sponge springs back when touched. If necessary, rotate the tin and finish baking for a further 2 minutes.

* Remove from the oven and leave to cool in the tins for 5 minutes before transferring to a metal cooling rack.

* Whilst the cupcakes are cooling, make the meringue frosting by combining the seven-minute frosting with the strawberry flavouring, if desired. Pipe onto the cupcakes and decorate with the sliced strawberries.

Coconut butter cupcakes
with white chocolate ganache

These delicately flavoured cupcakes get the double thumbs-up from Charlie, who likes them without the ganache. Personally, I think the white chocolate complements them really nicely. See what you think.

makes: **12 muffin-sized cupcakes**
preparation: **25 minutes**
baking: **25 minutes**
cooling: **35 minutes**
freeze: **Yes**

for the cupcake mixture
175g (6oz) dairy-free spread
175g (6oz) caster sugar
3 large eggs, beaten
175g (6oz) wheat-
    and gluten-free
    self-raising flour
1 tsp xanthan gum
1½ tsp gluten-free
    baking powder
50g (2oz) desiccated coconut
2 tbsp coconut cream

*for the white
    chocolate ganache*
115g (4oz) dairy-free
    white chocolate
125ml (4fl oz) soya
    double cream

equipment
12-hole muffin tin

* Preheat the oven to 180°C/160°C fan/Gas 4. Line the tin with muffin cases.

* In a large mixing bowl, use a hand-held electric mixer on a high speed setting to cream together the dairy-free spread and sugar for about 3 minutes until light and fluffy.

* Gradually add the beaten eggs on a medium speed setting, mixing well between each addition. Don't worry if the mixture curdles slightly; just turn the mixer setting up to high for a couple of seconds and the mixture will become smooth again.

* Fold in the sifted flour, xanthan gum and baking powder using a large metal spoon so you don't knock the air out.

* Add the desiccated coconut and coconut cream and carefully fold in until combined.

* Divide the mixture evenly among the muffin cases, filling each three-quarters full. I use a level ice-cream scoop of mixture, which ensures an equal amount in each case. The mixture is quite firm, so level with the back of a teaspoon.

* Bake in the middle of the oven for 20 minutes or until the cakes are well risen, golden and the sponge springs back when touched. If necessary, rotate the tin and finish baking for a further 2 minutes.

recipe continues...

* Remove from the oven and leave to cool in the tins for 5 minutes before transferring to a metal cooling rack.

* Whilst the cupcakes are cooling, make the ganache. Melt the chocolate and cream together in a heatproof bowl over a saucepan of boiling water taken off the heat. White chocolate is extremely difficult to melt, so it is important that you take the saucepan off the heat before placing the bowl on top. Stir continuously until the chocolate has melted and combined with the cream.

* Using a hand-held mixer on a high speed setting, beat the ganache until it becomes nice and light. Using a round-bladed knife, spread the cooled ganache over the top of the cupcakes.

* Store the cakes in an airtight container for up to two days.

Chocolate chip
& pistachio friands

makes: **10 muffin-sized cakes**
preparation: **30 minutes**
baking: **35 minutes**
cooling: **35 minutes**
freeze: **Yes**

150g (5½oz) pistachio
   nuts, shelled
60g (2¼oz) wheat- and
   gluten-free plain flour
½ tsp xanthan gum
175g (6oz) dairy-free spread
210g (7½oz) icing sugar
2 tbsp cocoa powder
½ tsp ground cardamom
5 large egg whites,
   at room temperature
200g (7oz) good-quality
   (60% cocoa) dark dairy-
   free chocolate chips
Icing sugar, to dust

equipment
12-hole muffin tin

tip: In Australia, the friands
are baked in small oval tins
without cases. These can be
difficult to find in the UK, so
I use muffin tins with cases.

If you really want to impress your friends when they drop round for coffee, pop these in the oven just before they arrive and serve them warm from the oven. The chocolate chips will be gooey and still melting and the hint of cardamom makes them glamorous and special.

* Preheat the oven to 200°C/180°C fan/Gas 6. Line the tin with paper cases.

* Toast the pistachios by spreading them out on a baking sheet and placing in the oven for 7 to 8 minutes. Remove from the oven and allow to cool.

* Place the cooled pistachio nuts, flour and xanthan gum into a food processor and process until finely ground.

* In a large mixing bowl, use a hand-held electric mixer on a high speed setting to cream the dairy-free spread and icing sugar together for about 3 minutes until light and fluffy.

* Sift together the flour and pistachios with the cocoa powder and ground cardamom and carefully fold into the creamed mixture.

* Lightly whisk the egg whites until they form a light floppy foam. Stir the egg whites and chocolate chips into the mixture until combined.

* Divide the mixture evenly among the cases, using an ice-cream scoop to ensure an equal amount in each case. Level the mixture with the back of a teaspoon.

* Bake in the oven for 25 to 30 minutes or until the cakes are just firm when touched. If necessary, rotate the tin and finish baking for a further few minutes.

* Remove the friands from the oven and cool in the tin for 5 minutes, then transfer to a metal cooling rack.

* Dust with icing sugar to serve. Store the friands in an airtight container for up to three days (do not keep in the fridge).

Coffee & pecan cupcakes

makes: **14 muffin-sized cupcakes**
preparation: **30 minutes**
baking: **25 minutes**
cooling: **35 minutes**
freeze: **You can freeze the cakes before icing them**

for the cupcake mixture
75g (2¾oz) pecan nuts
175g (6oz) dairy-free spread
175g (6oz) soft light brown sugar
3 large eggs, beaten
175g (6oz) wheat- and gluten-free self-raising flour
1 tsp xanthan gum
1½ tsp gluten-free baking powder
1½ tbsp instant coffee mixed with 2 tbsp boiling water
Chocolate coffee beans, for decoration

for the coffee frosting
2 tsp coffee essence or strong filter coffee
1 x Dairy-free Cream (see page 170) or Seven-minute Frosting (see page 167)

ingredients continue...

I know I have said before that I am not a great coffee lover, but for some reason I really love all coffee cakes. These beautifully moist cupcakes, with their light and airy frosting, look wonderful and are a real treat.

* Preheat the oven to 180°C/160°C fan/Gas 4. Line the tins with muffin cases.

* Toast all your pecan nuts by spreading them out on a baking sheet and placing in the oven for 7 to 8 minutes. Once toasted and cooled, finely chop and put to one side.

* In a mixing bowl and using a hand-held mixer on a high setting, cream the dairy-free spread and soft light brown sugar together for about 3 minutes until light and fluffy.

* Gradually add the beaten eggs on a medium speed setting, mixing well between each addition. Don't worry if the mixture curdles slightly; just turn the mixer setting up to high for a couple of seconds and the mixture will become smooth again.

* Fold in the sifted flour, xanthan gum and baking powder using a large metal spoon so you don't knock the air out. Add the coffee and pecan nuts, carefully folding in until the mixture is nice and smooth.

* Divide the mixture evenly among the muffin cases. Use a heaped ice-cream scoop full of mixture to ensure an equal amount in each case. Level the mixture with the back of a teaspoon.

* Bake in the oven for 20 to 25 minutes or until well risen and springy to the touch.

* Whilst the cakes are baking, make the coffee frosting by mixing the coffee essence into the cream or frosting.

* To make the syrup, place the coffee and sugar into a heatproof jug and pour in 25ml (1fl oz) boiling water, stirring briskly until the coffee and sugar have dissolved. This should take only a minute or so.

recipe continues...

for the coffee syrup
½ tbsp instant coffee
25g (1oz) demerara sugar

equipment
12- and 6-hole muffin tins

* Remove the cupcakes from the oven and leave in the tins. Prick them all over with a metal skewer or fork and spoon 2 teaspoons of coffee syrup over each cupcake. Leave the cupcakes for 5 minutes to soak up the syrup, then turn out onto a metal cooling rack.

* Once the cupcakes have cooled completely, pipe on the coffee frosting and decorate with chocolate coffee beans, if desired.

* Unfrosted cupcakes will keep for five days if stored in an airtight container (do not keep in the fridge). Frosted cupcakes should be eaten the same day.

Spicy apple cupcakes
with streusel topping

makes: **18 cupcakes**
preparation: **30 minutes**
baking: **30 minutes**
cooling: **35 minutes**
freeze: **No**

for the cake mixture
115g (4oz) dairy-free spread
215g (7½oz) granulated sugar
80g (3oz) soft light brown sugar
4 large eggs, beaten
300g (10½oz) wheat- and gluten-free self-raising flour
2 tsp xanthan gum
1 tsp bicarbonate of soda
¾ tsp salt

ingredients continue....

I wasn't sure whether to call these muffins or cupcakes – the apple sauce makes them wonderfully moist and the streusel topping dribbled with lemon glaze is satisfyingly crunchy.

* Preheat the oven to 180C/160°C fan/Gas 4. Line the tins with muffin cases.

* First make the streusel topping by placing all the ingredients in a mixing bowl and using your fingers to mix into a light crumb, then put to one side.

* In a large mixing bowl, use a hand-held electric mixer on a high setting to cream the dairy-free spread and both sugars for about 3 minutes until light and fluffy.

* Gradually add the eggs on a medium speed setting, mixing well between each addition. Don't worry if it curdles slightly; just turn up the mixer speed to high for a few seconds and the mixture will become smooth again.

* Fold in the sifted flour, xanthan gum, bicarbonate of soda, salt, cinnamon, nutmeg, cloves and apple sauce using a large metal spoon so you don't knock the air out.

recipe continues...

2 tsp ground cinnamon

½ tsp ground nutmeg

¼ tsp ground cloves

350g (12oz) unsweetened apple sauce (or tinned apple slices, whizzed into a purée in a food processor)

for the streusel topping

45g (1½oz) dairy-free spread

140g (5oz) wheat- and gluten-free plain flour

115g (4oz) soft light brown sugar

70g (2½oz) gluten-free porridge oats (see Key Ingredients, page 10)

½ tsp ground cinnamon

for the lemon glaze

100g (3½oz) icing sugar

1½ tbsp lemon juice

equipment

12- and 6-hole muffin tins

* Divide the mixture evenly among the prepared muffin cases. Use an ice-cream scoop of mixture, which ensures an equal amount in each cup. Level the mixture with the back of a teaspoon, then sprinkle the streusel topping evenly over each cupcake, pressing it down lightly into the mixture.

* Bake in the oven for 20 to 25 minutes or until a metal skewer inserted into the middle of the cakes comes out clean. If necessary, rotate the tins and finish baking for a further couple of minutes.

* Remove from the oven and leave to cool in the tins for 5 minutes, then remove from the tins and transfer to a metal cooling rack.

* Make the lemon glaze by mixing the icing sugar and lemon juice together, then drizzle lightly across the top of the cooled cupcakes. Store in an airtight container for three days (do not store in the fridge).

Drizzled honey cupcakes

makes: 12 muffin-sized
   cupcakes
preparation: 25 minutes
baking: 25 minutes
cooling: 35 minutes
freeze: Yes

for the cupcake mixture
170g (6oz) wheat-
   and gluten-free
   self-raising flour
1 tsp xanthan gum
½ tsp ground cinnamon
¼ tsp ground cloves
¼ tsp ground nutmeg
180g (6½oz) dairy-free spread
170g (6oz) caster sugar
2 tbsp runny honey
4 large eggs, beaten
Grated zest of 2
   medium oranges

for the walnut topping
15g (½oz) walnut pieces,
   finely chopped
¼ tsp ground cinnamon
2 tbsp runny honey
Juice of 1 orange

equipment
12-hole muffin tin

tip: If you like a bit of crunch
in your cake as well as on
top, add 40g (1½oz) finely
chopped walnuts to the
mixture when you are folding
in the flour and spices.

These little cakes are so sweet and sticky and because they don't have a frosting, they make a great addition to packed lunches or picnics.

* Preheat the oven to 180°C/160°C fan/Gas 4. Line the tin with muffin cases.

* Toast the walnuts in the oven for 6 minutes. Sift the flour, xanthan gum, cinnamon, ground cloves and nutmeg together in a bowl and put to one side.

* In a large mixing bowl, use a hand-held electric mixer on a high speed setting to cream together the dairy-free spread and sugar for about 3 minutes until light and fluffy.

* Gradually add the honey, beaten eggs and orange zest on a medium speed setting, mixing well between each addition. Don't worry if the mixture curdles slightly, just turn the mixer setting up to high for a couple of seconds and the mixture will become smooth again.

* Fold in the sifted flour mixture using a large metal spoon so you don't knock the air out.

* Divide the mixture evenly among the muffin cases, filling each three-quarters full. I use a level ice-cream scoop of mixture, which ensures an equal amount in each case. The mixture is quite firm, so level with the back of a teaspoon.

* Bake in the middle of the oven for 20 minutes or until the cakes are well risen, golden and the sponge springs back when touched. If necessary, rotate the tin and finish baking for a further 2 minutes.

* Whilst the cakes are in the oven, make the topping. Mix together the finely chopped walnuts and cinnamon. Put the honey and orange juice in a heavy-based saucepan and heat gently, stirring until combined.

* Remove the cupcakes from the oven and leave to cool in the tins for 5 minutes before transferring to a metal cooling rack.

* Whilst the cupcakes are still warm, prick the tops with a metal skewer or fork and drizzle the warm honey and orange mixture over them. Sprinkle the tops of the cakes with the cinnamon-coated chopped walnuts. Serve warm or cold.

* The cupcakes will keep for five days if stored in an airtight container (do not keep in the fridge).

Carrot cupcakes
with coconut & orange frosting

makes: 18 muffin-sized
   cupcakes
preparation: 25 minutes
baking: 25 minutes
cooling: 35 minutes
freeze: Yes

for the cupcake mixture
100g (3½oz) pecan nuts
225g (8oz) dairy-free spread
225g (8oz) soft light
   brown sugar
Finely grated zest of
   1 orange
4 large eggs, beaten
225g (8oz) wheat-
   and gluten-free
   self-raising flour
1 tsp xanthan gum
1 tsp ground mixed spice
150g (5½oz) carrots,
   finely grated
75g (2¾oz) sultanas

*for the coconut
   and orange frosting*
225g (8oz) virgin coconut oil
Zest and juice of 1 orange
2 tbsp soya/rice/almond milk
450g (1lb) icing sugar

equipment
12- and 6-hole muffin tins

Perhaps it's because these cupcakes contain carrot, but I always think of them as being healthy cakes. Without the frosting, they make a delicious snack that can be popped into a lunchbox without any guilt. With the frosting, they become a guilty treat!

* Preheat the oven to 180°C/160°C fan/Gas 4. Line the tins with muffin cases.

* Toast the pecans nuts by spreading them out on a baking sheet and placing in the oven for 7 to 8 minutes. Once toasted, chop and put to one side.

* In a large mixing bowl, use a hand-held electric mixer on a high speed setting to cream together the dairy-free spread, sugar and grated orange zest for about 3 minutes until light and fluffy.

* Gradually add the beaten eggs on a medium speed setting, mixing well between each addition. Don't worry if the mixture curdles slightly; just turn the mixer setting up to high for a couple of seconds and the mixture will become smooth again.

* Fold in the sifted flour, xanthan gum, mixed spice, chopped pecans, grated carrot and sultanas using a large metal spoon so you don't knock the air out.

* Divide the mixture evenly among the muffin cases, filling each three-quarters full. I use a heaped ice-cream scoop of mixture, which ensures an equal amount in each case. The mixture is quite firm, so level with the back of a teaspoon.

* Bake in the middle of the oven for 20 minutes or until the cakes are well risen and the sponge springs back when touched. If necessary, rotate the tin and finish baking for a further 2 minutes.

recipe continues...

* Remove from the oven and leave to cool in the tins for 5 minutes before transferring to a metal cooling rack.

* Whilst the cupcakes are cooling, make the coconut and orange frosting. Using a hand-held mixer on a medium setting, beat the coconut oil until soft and smooth. Depending on your room temperature, the oil can be quite hard, so you need to start beating it slowly. It will gradually soften and become creamy.

* Add the orange zest, juice and milk and continue to beat. Gradually add the icing sugar (if you put too much in to start with, you could end up spraying it all over yourself). If the finished frosting feels too stiff, add a little more milk until you reach a smooth consistency. If it is too soft, add a little more icing sugar. The consistency needs to be firm enough to pipe onto the cakes and hold its shape.

* Pipe the frosting onto the cakes and decorate. Store the cupcakes in an airtight container for up to five days.

tip: Remember to finely grate the carrot for the cupcakes. Coarsely grated carrot will produce a lumpy and uneven cupcake.

Spiced courgette cupcakes
with orange glacé icing

A wonderfully moist and wholesome cupcake that makes use of those few courgettes left in the vegetable rack. Just because a cake is wholesome, doesn't mean it can't be delicious, and topped with a simple orange glaze these really are moreish.

makes: 12 cupcakes
preparation: 30 minutes
baking: 30 minutes
cooling: 35 minutes
freeze: Yes

for the cupcake mixture
45g (1½oz) walnuts
215g (7½oz) wheat-
    and gluten-free
    self-raising flour
1 tsp xanthan gum
½ tsp bicarbonate of soda
¼ tsp gluten-free
    baking powder
½ tsp salt
1 tsp ground cinnamon
¼ tsp ground nutmeg
Pinch of ground cloves
160g (5½oz) soft light
    brown sugar
100ml (3½fl oz) vegetable oil
1 large egg
½ tbsp vanilla extract
½ tsp grated lemon zest
325g (11½oz) courgettes,
    finely grated

for the orange glacé mixture
100g (3½oz) icing sugar
1 tbsp freshly squeezed
    orange juice

equipment
12-hole muffin tin

* Preheat the oven to 180°C/160°C fan/Gas 4. Line the tin with muffin cases.

* Toast the walnuts by spreading them out on a baking sheet and placing them in the oven for 7 to 8 minutes. Once toasted and cooled, finely chop and put to one side.

* In a mixing bowl, mix together the flour, xanthan gum, bicarbonate of soda, gluten-free baking powder, salt, cinnamon, nutmeg and cloves. Sift into another mixing bowl.

* In a large mixing bowl, use a large balloon whisk to beat together the sugar, oil, egg, vanilla and zest until well combined and smooth. Stir in the grated courgette.

* Gradually fold in the flour mixture and chopped nuts using a large metal spoon until just combined.

* Divide the mixture evenly among the prepared muffin cups. Use a level ice-cream scoop of mixture, which ensures an equal amount in each cup. Level the mixture with the back of a teaspoon.

* Bake in the oven for 20 to 25 minutes or until a metal skewer inserted into the middle of the cakes comes out clean. If necessary, rotate the tins and finish baking for a further couple of minutes.

* Remove from the oven and leave to cool in the tins for 5 minutes, then remove from the tins and transfer to a metal cooling rack.

* Make the glacé icing by mixing the icing sugar and orange juice together, then spoon onto the cooled cupcakes and level with a round-bladed knife.

* Store in an airtight container for three days (do not store in the fridge).

White chocolate
& raspberry muffins

makes: **10 to 12 muffins**
preparation: **30 minutes**
baking: **30 minutes**
cooling: **35 minutes**
freeze: **No**

225g (8oz) wheat-
   and gluten-free
   self-raising flour
1 tsp xanthan gum
2 tsp gluten-free
   baking powder
½ tsp bicarbonate of soda
115g (4oz) caster sugar
80g (3oz) dairy-free spread,
   melted and cooled
225ml (8fl oz) soya yoghurt
1 large egg, beaten
80g (3oz) dairy-free white
   chocolate, chips or
   roughly chopped
½ tsp vanilla extract
150g (5½oz) raspberries

equipment
12-hole muffin tin

For years I tried to make muffins and was never very successful, and then the penny dropped! When recipes say don't overmix, they really mean it. Just fold in eight or nine times and don't worry if some of the ingredients haven't been combined. Bingo – perfect muffins every time!

* Preheat the oven to 180°C/160°C fan/Gas 4. Line the tin with muffin cases.

* In a large bowl, sift together the flour, xanthan gum, baking powder, bicarbonate of soda and sugar. Make a well in the centre.

* Quickly and carefully add the melted and cooled dairy-free spread, yoghurt, egg, white chocolate and vanilla extract.

* Using a large metal spoon, fold the ingredients together until just combined. Don't overmix otherwise the muffins will have a rubbery texture. Gently fold in the raspberries so you don't break them.

* Divide the mixture evenly among the cases. I use an ice-cream scoop of mixture, which ensures an equal amount in each case. Level the mixture with the back of a teaspoon.

* Bake in the oven for 30 minutes or until they are well risen and springy to the touch. Remove from the oven and leave to cool in the tin for 5 minutes, then transfer to a metal cooling rack.

* These muffins really are best eaten on the day they are baked, but will store for a couple of days in an airtight container (do not keep in the fridge).

Gingerbread cupcakes
with lemon glaze

makes: **14 muffin-sized cupcakes**
preparation: **30 minutes**
baking: **25 minutes**
cooling: **40 minutes**
freeze: **Yes**

Although these little cakes are not as dark and dense as a gingerbread traybake, they are still gorgeously sticky. With the zingy lemon glaze, I bet you can't eat one without having to constantly lick your fingers!

for the cupcake mixture
115g (4oz) dairy-free spread
300g (10oz) wheat- and gluten-free self-raising flour
1 tsp xanthan gum
1 tbsp gluten-free baking powder
4 tsp ground ginger
1 tsp ground cinnamon
225g (8oz) soft light brown sugar
2 large eggs, beaten
115ml (4fl oz) runny honey
175ml (6fl oz) soya/rice/almond milk
2 tbsp glacé ginger

for the lemon glaze
60g (2¼oz) icing sugar
2½ tbsp lemon juice

equipment
12- and 6-hole muffin tins

* Preheat the oven to 195°C/175°C fan/Gas 5. Line the tins with muffin cases.

* In a heavy-based saucepan over a gentle heat, melt the dairy-free spread. Once melted, put to one side.

* Sift the flour, xanthan gum, baking powder, ginger and cinnamon into a mixing bowl and put to one side.

* In another large mixing bowl using a large balloon whisk, mix the sugar, eggs, honey, melted dairy-free spread and milk together until combined.

* Gradually and carefully fold in the flour mixture in three stages using a large metal spoon so you don't knock the air out. Carefully fold in the glacé ginger.

* Divide the batter evenly among the muffin cases, filling each three-quarters full. I use an ice-cream scoop of mixture, which ensures an equal amount in each case. Level the mixture with the back of a teaspoon.

* Bake in the oven for 20 to 25 minutes or until the cakes are well risen and a metal skewer inserted into the middle of a cake comes out clean.

* Remove from the oven and leave to cool in the tins for 10 minutes before transferring to a metal cooling rack.

* To make the glaze, sift the icing sugar into a bowl and slowly add the lemon juice, stirring until well combined. Drizzle the glaze over the tops of the cupcakes. Store the cakes in an airtight container for up to five days (do not store in the fridge).

Cappuccino cupcakes
with white chocolate ganache

makes: 12 to 14 cupcakes
preparation: 30 minutes
baking: 30 minutes
cooling: 50 minutes
freeze: Yes

for the cupcake mixture
225g (8oz) dairy-free spread
225g (8oz) golden
   caster sugar
4 large eggs, beaten
3 tbsp instant coffee
   granules dissolved in
   2 tbsp hot water, cooled
175g (6oz) wheat- and
   gluten-free plain flour
1 tsp xanthan gum
1 tsp gluten-free
   baking powder
50g (2oz) ground almonds
Grated dark dairy-free
   chocolate, for decoration

for the white
   chocolate ganache
100g (3½oz) dairy-free
   white chocolate
75ml (2½fl oz) soya
   double cream
1 tsp vanilla extract

equipment
12- and 6-hole muffin tins

I love these cupcakes with their fudgy ganache topping, but they taste just as good with a white chocolate frosting dusted with cocoa powder.

* Preheat the oven to 180°C/160°C fan/Gas 4. Line the tins with muffin cases. In a large mixing bowl, use a hand-held electric mixer on a high setting to cream the dairy-free spread and sugar together for about 3 minutes until light and fluffy.

* Gradually add the eggs and the dissolved coffee on a medium speed setting, mixing well between each addition. Don't worry if it curdles slightly; just turn up the mixer speed to high for a few seconds and the mixture will become smooth again.

* Fold in the sifted flour, xanthan gum, baking powder and ground almonds using a large metal spoon so you don't knock the air out. Don't worry if the final mixture looks slightly grainy and curdled.

* Divide the mixture evenly among the cases. Use a heaped ic-cream scoop full of mixture, which ensures an equal amount in each case. Level the mixture with the back of a teaspoon.

* Bake for 20 to 25 minutes or until the cakes are well risen and the sponge springs back when touched. If necessary, rotate the tins and finish baking for a further couple of minutes. Remove from the oven and leave to cool in the tins for 5 minutes, then transfer to a metal cooling rack.

* To make the ganache, place the white chocolate in a heatproof bowl and place it over a saucepan of water that has just boiled. Take the saucepan off the heat completely and keep stirring the chocolate until it has melted and is nice and smooth.

* Whip the cream for a couple of minutes until it is nice and smooth, then add to the melted chocolate along with the vanilla extract. Stir until fully combined. Using a round-bladed knife, smooth the ganache evenly over the cupcakes. Pop the cupcakes into the fridge until the ganache has set. Decorate with grated dark chocolate.

tip: Store the cupcakes in an airtight container for up to five days (but not in the fridge).

Passion fruit cupcakes
with passion fruit butter

makes: **12 cupcakes**
preparation: **30 minutes**
baking: **30 minutes**
cooling: **35 minutes**
freeze: **No**

6 passion fruit
200g (7oz) dairy-free spread
200g (7oz) caster sugar
Grated zest of 2 lemons
4 large eggs, beaten
200g (7oz) wheat-
    and gluten-free
    self-raising flour
2 tsp xanthan gum
Icing sugar, for dusting
1 x Passion Fruit Butter
    (see page 169)

equipment
12-hole muffin tin

I could eat spoonfuls of passion fruit butter on its own – it is just so delicious. It also tastes good as a filling, sandwiched in a layered cupcake and gently dusted with icing sugar, yum!

* Preheat the oven to 180C/160°C fan/Gas 4. Filled and layered cupcakes work much better when baked without muffin cases, so brush the muffin tin with dairy-free spread and dust with flour, tapping out the excess.

* Halve the passion fruit and scoop out the pulp. Place in a food processor to loosen the pips. Strain through a sieve, collecting the juice in a bowl, then put to one side.

* In a large mixing bowl, use a hand-held electric mixer on a high setting to cream the dairy-free spread, sugar and grated lemon zest together for about 3 minutes until light and fluffy.

* Gradually add the eggs on a medium speed setting, mixing well between each addition. Don't worry if it curdles slightly; just turn up the mixer speed to high for a few seconds and the mixture will become smooth again. Fold in the sifted flour, xanthan gum and passion fruit juice using a large metal spoon so you don't knock the air out.

* Divide the mixture evenly among the prepared muffin cups. Use a level ice-cream scoop of mixture, which ensures an equal amount in each cup. Level the mixture with the back of a teaspoon.

* Bake in the oven for 20 to 25 minutes or until the cakes are well risen and golden and the sponge springs back when touched. If necessary, rotate the tins and finish baking for a further couple of minutes.

* Remove from the oven and leave to cool in the tins for 5 minutes, then remove from the cups and transfer to a metal cooling rack. Once the cupcakes have cooled, use a serrated knife to gently cut the tops off the cakes and put to one side.

* Spoon 1 tablespoon of the passion fruit butter onto each cupcake bottom, then replace the tops. Dust with the icing sugar. Store the cakes in an airtight container for three days (do not store in the fridge).

Hummingbird cupcakes
with marmalade frosting

makes: **12 muffin-sized cupcakes**
preparation: **25 minutes**
baking: **25 minutes**
cooling: **1 hour 15 minutes**
freeze: **You can freeze the cakes before icing them**

for the cake mixture
60g (2¼oz) walnuts
120g (4½oz) dairy-free spread
200g (7oz) caster sugar
1 tsp vanilla extract
2 large eggs, beaten
300g (10½oz) ripe bananas, mashed (2 small bananas)
200g (7oz) tinned crushed pineapple in fruit juice, drained (or chopped pineapple whizzed into a paste in a food processor)
60g (2¼oz) desiccated coconut
225g (8oz) wheat- and gluten-free self-raising flour
1 tsp xanthan gum
½ tsp bicarbonate of soda
½ tsp ground cinnamon
½ tsp salt

ingredients continue...

I have always loved baking cakes for family and friends to help celebrate special occasions, birthdays, anniversaries and Mother's Day, and these cheerful and fragrant cupcakes make a truly wonderful gift. Dress them up with big white and yellow daisies or experiment with thinly sliced fresh pineapple, dried in the oven for 30 minutes and then left to dry into shape in muffin tins. Let your imagination run riot.

* Preheat the oven to 180°C/160°C fan/Gas 4. Line the tin with muffin cases.

* Toast the walnuts by spreading them out on a baking sheet and placing in the oven for 7 to 8 minutes. Once toasted, chop and put to one side.

* In a large mixing bowl, use a hand-held electric mixer on a high speed setting to cream together the dairy-free spread, sugar and vanilla extract for about 3 minutes until light and fluffy.

* Gradually add the beaten eggs on a medium speed setting, mixing well between each addition. Don't worry if the mixture curdles slightly; just turn the mixer setting up to high for a couple of seconds and the mixture will become smooth again.

* In another bowl, mix together the mashed bananas, pineapple, chopped walnuts and coconut. Add to the egg mixture and beat until combined.

* Fold in the sifted flour, xanthan gum, bicarbonate of soda, cinnamon and salt using a large metal spoon so you don't knock the air out.

* Divide the mixture evenly among the muffin cases, filling each three-quarters full. I use a heaped ice-cream scoop of mixture, which ensures an equal amount in each case. The mixture is quite firm, so level with the back of a teaspoon.

* Bake in the middle of the oven for 20 minutes or until the cakes are well risen and the sponge springs back when touched. If necessary, rotate the tin and finish baking for a further 2 minutes.

recipe continues...

for the marmalade frosting

60g (2¼oz) coconut oil
60g (2¼oz) dairy-free spread
Juice of ½ orange
1 heaped tbsp coarse-cut
    marmalade
240g (8oz) icing sugar

equipment
12-hole muffin tin

....

tip: If you like lots of frosting, double the frosting quantities and chill in the fridge for an hour before swirling onto the cupcakes.

* Remove from the oven and leave to cool in the tin for 5 minutes before transferring to a metal cooling rack.

* Whilst the cupcakes are cooling, make the marmalade frosting. Using a hand mixer on a medium setting, beat the coconut oil until soft and smooth. Depending on your room temperature, the oil can be quite hard so you need to start beating it slowly. It will gradually soften and become creamy.

* Add the dairy-free spread and orange juice and beat until smooth. Gradually add the icing sugar (if you put too much in to start with, you could end up spraying it all over yourself). Beat until smooth. Don't worry if it feels a bit runny, it will firm up when chilling in the fridge. Stir the marmalade in so it is evenly distributed throughout the frosting.

* Place the frosting into the fridge to chill and firm for 40 minutes. Spoon the frosting onto the cupcakes and swirl with a palette knife (you won't be able to pipe the frosting on because of the orange peel in the marmalade).

* Decorate as required. Store in an airtight container for up to three days.

Vanilla cupcakes

makes: **12 muffin-sized cupcakes**
preparation: **25 minutes**
baking: **25 minutes**
cooling: **35 minutes**
freeze: **Yes**

for the cupcake mixture
4 large eggs, beaten
3 tsp vanilla extract
200g (7oz) dairy-free spread
200g (7oz) caster sugar
200g (7oz) wheat- and gluten-free self-raising flour
2 tsp xanthan gum

for the vanilla frosting
225g (8oz) virgin coconut oil
4 tsp golden vanilla extract
Zest and juice of 1 lemon
2 tbsp soya/rice/almond milk
475g (1lb 1oz) icing sugar

equipment
12-hole muffin tin

tip: Raising agents react much more slowly these days, so if you want to make double or treble the quantity but don't have enough tins, don't worry. You can prepare your mixture in one go, keep the extra covered until you are ready, then divide into the cases and pop into the oven.

As a child I always loved cupcakes – it didn't matter what the flavour, I had a beautiful little cake all to myself. So it only seemed right that my very first attempt at dairy-, wheat- and gluten-free baking was with a vanilla cupcake.

* Preheat the oven to 180°C/160°C fan/Gas 4. Line the muffin tin with muffin cases. Blend the eggs and vanilla together with a fork and put to one side. In a large mixing bowl, use a hand-held electric mixer on a high speed setting to cream together the dairy-free spread and sugar for about 3 minutes until light and fluffy.

* Gradually add the beaten eggs and vanilla extract on a medium speed setting, mixing well between each addition. Don't worry if the mixture curdles slightly; just turn the mixer setting up to high for a couple of seconds and the mixture will become smooth again. Fold in the sifted flour and xanthan gum using a large metal spoon so you don't knock the air out.

* Divide the mixture evenly among the muffin cases, filling each three-quarters full. I use a level ice-cream scoop of mixture, which ensures an equal amount in each case. The mixture is quite firm, so level with the back of a teaspoon.

* Bake in the middle of the oven for 20 minutes or until the cakes are well risen, golden and the sponge springs back when touched. If necessary, rotate the tin and finish baking for a further 2 minutes.

* Remove from the oven and leave to cool in the tins for 5 minutes before transferring to a metal cooling rack.

* Whilst the cupcakes are cooling, make the frosting. Using a hand-held mixer on a medium setting, beat the coconut oil until smooth. The oil can be quite hard so you need to start beating it slowly. It will gradually soften and become creamy.

* Add the vanilla extract, lemon zest and juice and milk and continue to beat. Gradually add the icing sugar (if you put too much in to start with, you could spray it all over yourself). If the finished frosting feels too stiff, add a little more milk until you reach a smooth consistency. If it is too soft, add a little more icing sugar. The consistency needs to be firm enough to hold its shape.

* Pipe the frosting onto the cooled cupcakes and decorate as required.

Peanut butter cupcakes

makes: **18 muffin-sized cupcakes**
preparation: **25 minutes**
baking: **30 minutes**
cooling: **35 minutes**
freeze: **Yes**

for the cupcake mixture
4 large eggs, beaten
2 tsp vanilla extract
240g (8oz) wheat-and gluten-free self-raising flour
2 tsp xanthan gum
¼ tsp salt
150g (5½oz) dairy-free spread
260g (9oz) smooth peanut butter
375g (13oz) soft dark brown sugar
125ml (4fl oz) soya/rice/almond milk

for the peanut butter mixture
65g (2¼oz) smooth peanut butter
50g (2oz) dairy-free spread
2 tsp vanilla extract
3 tbsp soya/rice/almond milk
325g (11½oz) icing sugar

equipment
12- and 6-hole muffin tins

I just love these cakes and can quite happily eat spoonfuls of the frosting on its own! Of course, you can always top the cakes with chocolate frosting if you prefer – both work equally well.

* Preheat the oven to 180°C/160°C fan/Gas 4. Line the tins with muffin cases. To make the cupcakes, blend the eggs and vanilla extract together with a fork and put to one side.

* Sift the flour, xanthan gum and salt together into a bowl and put to one side.

* In a large mixing bowl, use a hand-held electric mixer on a high speed setting to cream together the dairy-free spread, peanut butter and sugar for about 3 minutes until lighter in colour and fluffy.

* Gradually add the beaten eggs and vanilla extract on a medium speed setting, mixing well between each addition. Don't worry if the mixture curdles slightly; just turn the mixer setting up to high for a couple of seconds and the mixture will become smooth again.

* Fold a third of the flour gently into the mixture using a large metal spoon, then fold in a third of the milk. Repeat, alternating the flour and milk, until all ingredients have been combined.

* Divide the mixture evenly among the muffin cases, filling each three-quarters full. I use a level ice-cream scoop of mixture, which ensures an equal amount in each case.

* Bake in the middle of the oven for 20 to 25 minutes or until the cakes are well risen and the sponge springs back when touched. If necessary, rotate the tins and finish baking for a further 2 minutes.

* Remove from the oven and leave to cool in the tins for 5 minutes before transferring to a metal cooling rack.

* Whilst the cupcakes are cooling, make the frosting. In a large mixing bowl, use a hand-held mixer on a high setting to cream the peanut butter, dairy-free spread and vanilla extract until smooth.

* Slowly beat in the milk and icing sugar until thick and creamy. If the mixture is too stiff, add a little more milk. If it is too runny, add a little more icing sugar until you have the right consistency.

* Pipe the frosting onto the cooled cupcakes and decorate as required.

The Art of Decoration

Part of the pleasure of baking for me is in the final presentation. If I have the time, I love nothing more than planning what decorations and colours I am going to use. After all, any lovingly prepared cake deserves to be presented in a suitably proper manner. Take inspiration from books and paintings, browse the internet and look at flowers in your garden – nature's colours are amazing and the combinations are sometimes surprising. Let your imagination run riot.

Whilst there are entire books dedicated to the art of decorating cakes, I have suggested just a few simple ideas from which you can create literally thousands of combinations and finishes.

Swirls of creamy frosting are not difficult to achieve and the beauty of them are that the less uniform and complicated they are, the more charming they become. Finish with a scattering of edible glitter and you are sure to draw gasps of awe and amazement.

Supermarkets and specialist cake decorating companies stock a wealth of sprinkles, sugar flowers and cake toppers, but do read the ingredients labels carefully, as a lot of supermarket decorations contain wheat starch. If you have time, it is fun to make your own and you can buy ready-to-roll icing, tinting it with a variety of colour pastes and liquids, whilst cutters can be bought from good cookery supply shops. I use Sugarflair colour pastes, which can be purchased from good cake decorating shops or online from the stockists listed below. Dr. Oetker has natural red and natural yellow liquid food colourings, free from artificial colours and preservatives, and providing a more subtle shade of colour. These can be purchased from most supermarkets.

Ready-to-roll icing now makes it very easy to create your own cake decorations. Browse the internet for different shape cutters and moulds and start making your own collection.

* Bright and cheerful flowers sit beautifully on top of any cake – think different sizes and contrasting colours. At Cake Angels, our signature celebration cake has a large funky daisy offset with a sprinkling of smaller flowers across the top and sides. Every cake we decorate is different and unique and all are created with a few simple cutters.
* Simple fun and funky shapes such as circles, hearts and stars look great in bright primary colours scattered over a white or contrasting background. Think Emma Bridgewater.

* Personalize cakes with alphabet and number cutters, creating simple messages or birthday greetings.
* Children love to pipe icing swirls and squiggles on to cupcakes. Somehow it doesn't matter a bit that the lines are wobbly because you know someone has been giggling and having fun.

Dark, milk or white chocolate can be used to make some fabulous finishing touches.
* Chocolate curls are made by holding a swivel-bladed vegetable peeler close to the edge of a bar of dairy-free chocolate and running along the top of the bar to shave off the curls. If the chocolate is too hard, the curls will be small and prone to flaking. Warm in a microwave for a few seconds before trying again.
* Chocolate shapes are made by pouring a thin layer of melted chocolate onto a baking parchment-lined baking tray and leaving to semi set. Using your choice of cutter stars, squares or circles, push into the chocolate and remove the cut-out shape. You could also use a sharp knife, first warmed in boiling water and wiped dry, to cut the chocolate into different shapes.
* Chocolate leaves require a delicate hand. Using a small paintbrush, paint melted chocolate onto the back of a clean dry leaf. Leave to set before carefully peeling the leaf away from the chocolate.

Fresh flowers can look stunning and are a simple way of creating a wonderfully romantic finish.
* Fresh rose petals strewn over the top of a cake look perfect. Use the small inner ones and make sure they are home grown without any pesticides.
* Crystallized flowers are simple to prepare. Choose edible varieties such as violets, pansies or primroses, brush with a little egg white and dust with caster sugar. Leave them to crisp on a wire cooling rack in a warm, dry place like an airing cupboard for a couple of hours.

Fresh berries can look amazing piled high on top of a Victoria sponge, on a chocolate cake or scattered across a frosted cupcake.
* Red berries in season look so delicious sitting on a bed of dairy-free cream frosting. Try to choose evenly sized fruit. Mixing your choice of berries can add colour and texture.
* Crystallized berries look especially pretty on a Fraisier cake. Brush fresh redcurrants and raspberries with a little egg white and dust with caster sugar. Leave them to stand on a wire cooling rack for a couple of hours in a warm, dry place like an airing cupboard.

Toppings, Frostings & Fillings

Why is it that everyone assumes frostings and fillings can be delicious only if they are made from butter and cream? Well, I can assure you this isn't the case. I am constantly being asked, 'How do you make your frostings so delicious?' or, 'Can I have the recipe?' and these are from people who love butter! Although I have suggested what topping or frosting to use with a particular cake, please feel free to experiment. Top the coconut cupcakes with rich chocolate frosting or fill a Victoria sponge with dairy-free cream and passion fruit butter. Let your imagination run wild and indulge your secret desires. After all, you deserve it.

Dairy-free condensed milk

Dare I say it, the Holy Grail of dairy-free baking! Once I discovered I could make my own condensed milk with dried soya milk powder, there was no stopping me. Any toffee-based recipes that up until then had been off limits, were now mine to enjoy. I have also discovered that you can get dried almond milk powder, so those who can't tolerate soya can also join the party. The powder is expensive, but a tin will make several batches of condensed milk and will keep in the store cupboard for up to two months after opening.

Makes About 400ml (14fl oz)
Preparation 20 minutes
Cooling 1 hour

Ingredients
55g (2oz) dairy-free spread
155g (5½oz) caster sugar
125g (4½oz) dried soya milk powder
½ tsp vanilla extract

Method
* Gently melt the dairy-free spread in a small heavy-based saucepan over a low heat. Remove from the heat when melted.
* Pour 110ml (3½fl oz) boiling water into a food processor. Add the melted spread, caster sugar, dried soya milk powder and vanilla extract. Blend until all ingredients are combined.
* Pour into a covered container and chill in the fridge for 1 hour before using.

Tip: The milk can be stored in an airtight container in the fridge for up to two weeks, just stir before using.

Seven minute frosting

Sometimes referred to as American frosting, this meringue-like topping is a wonderful base for flavours such as coffee, vanilla, strawberry, orange or rose water. You will need a sugar thermometer, as it is important that the sugar syrup reaches the right temperature before it is added to the egg whites.

Makes Enough to frost 18 cupcakes
Preparation 20 minutes
Freezing No

Ingredients
100g (3½oz) caster sugar, plus ½ tbsp
½ tbsp golden syrup
2 large egg whites

Method
* In a medium-sized heavy-based saucepan, combine the sugar, 50ml (2fl oz) water and the golden syrup. Clip the sugar thermometer to the side of the saucepan with the tip just touching the ingredients.
* Bring to the boil over a medium heat, stirring occasionally until the sugar dissolves. Continue to boil, without stirring, until the syrup reaches 110°C (225°F).
* Whilst the syrup is coming to boil and using a handheld electric mixer on a medium setting, whisk the egg whites until soft peaks form. Gradually add the ½ tbsp sugar, whisking until combined.
* Once the syrup has reached 110°C (225°F), remove from the heat and gradually pour onto the egg whites, whilst still whisking on a medium speed. Gradually increase the speed to high and continue to whisk the mixture until the bottom of the bowl is cool and the egg whites form stiff, but not dry, peaks. This will take about 7 minutes.
* If adding a flavour, add at this stage and whisk until combined. Use immediately, piping onto cupcakes or smoothing onto cakes.

Chocolate frosting

Who doesn't love chocolate frosting, swirled onto cupcakes or used to fill rich, luscious sponges. The beauty of this frosting is the melted chocolate – it gives it a depth and richness that cocoa powder alone just can't match.

Makes Enough to frost 18 cupcakes or fill
 a 20cm (8 inch) sponge
Preparation 10 minutes
Freezing Yes
Defrosting 3 to 4 hours at room temperature
 or overnight

Ingredients
115g (4oz) good-quality (60% cocoa)
 dark dairy-free chocolate
115g (4oz) dairy-free spread
2-3 tbsp soya/rice/almond milk
1 tsp vanilla extract
360g (12oz) icing sugar
1 tbsp cocoa powder

Method
* Melt the chocolate by placing it in a heatproof bowl over a simmering saucepan of water. Make sure the bottom of the bowl does not touch the water. Once melted, stir and remove from the heat. If you have a microwave, you can place the chocolate in a heatproof bowl and heat for 1½ minutes. Remove and stir the chocolate until it has completely melted.

* In a large mixing bowl, use a hand-held electric mixer on high to cream the dairy-free spread. Once smooth, beat in the milk and vanilla extract.

* Beat in the melted chocolate until smooth. Slowly beat in the icing sugar and cocoa until thick and creamy. If the mixture is too stiff, add a little more milk.

* Store in an airtight container in the fridge for 3 days.

Lemon curd

I have been known to eat spoonfuls of this zingy lemon curd straight out of the jar – it is just so delicious and totally addictive. You can happily layer it in ice cream sundaes, spread it on toast or fold a small amount into the Dairy-free Cream (see page 170) to serve alongside summer desserts.

Makes Enough to fill 12 Lemon Butterfly Cakes or
 a 20cm (8 inch) sponge
Preparation 25 minutes
Cooling 2 hours
Freezing Yes
Defrosting 3 to 4 hours at room temperature or
 overnight

Ingredients
3 large eggs
100g (3½oz) runny honey
Grated zest of 1 large lemon
175g (6oz) coconut oil
110ml (3½fl oz) lemon juice (about 5 small lemons)
50g (2oz) dairy-free spread

Method
* In a medium-sized heavy-based saucepan, use a large balloon whisk to combine the eggs, honey and lemon zest (do not heat at this stage). Add the coconut oil in small clumps so it will melt more evenly, then add the lemon juice.

* Whisk all the ingredients together over a medium heat until the coconut oil has melted, continuing to whisk until the mixture thickens and starts to bubble. Remove from the heat and pour through a fine sieve set over a medium-sized mixing bowl to strain the curd. Gradually whisk in the dairy-free spread until combined.

* Place in the fridge for 1 hour to thicken. Store in an airtight container in the fridge for up to a week.

Tip: The curd can be frozen. Defrost at room temperature for 3 or 4 hours before use.

Passion fruit butter

Passion fruit have a wonderful fruity and zesty flavour and the butter works beautifully as a filling for cakes or swirled into the Dairy-free Cream (see page 170). In fact, you can use it just like you would the lemon curd.

Makes Enough to fill 12 cupcakes or a 20cm (8 inch) sponge
Preparation 25 minutes
Cooling 1 hour
Freezing Yes
Defrosting 3 to 4 hours at room temperature or overnight

Ingredients
11 passion fruit
2 large eggs
2 large egg yolks
150g (5½oz) caster sugar
100g (3½oz) dairy-free spread

Method
* Put the seed pulp of 10 passion fruit into a food processor and whizz just to loosen the seeds. Strain into a jug.

* In a large mixing bowl and using a hand-held electric mixer on a high speed setting, cream together the eggs, egg yolks and sugar until thick and creamy.

* Melt the dairy-free spread in a small heavy-based saucepan over a gentle heat. When melted, stir in the egg mixture and passion fruit juice. Keep cooking, gently stirring constantly, for about 15 to 20 minutes until thickened.

* Take off the heat and whisk in the pulp of the last passion fruit.

* Place in the fridge for 1 hour to chill.

* Store in an airtight container in the fridge for up to one week.

Pomegranate molasses

Not only are pomegranates packed with polyphenol antioxidants, which help neutralize free radicals, they also make a delicious molasses, which can be used in sauces, casseroles and marinades. Normally associated with Middle Eastern cuisine, the molasses can also be used to drizzle over ice cream, as a base for cordials and, for baking. You can buy it in some supermarkets and specialist delis, but it is expensive, so make your own and store the extra in the fridge for future use.

Makes About 200ml (7fl oz)
Preparation 1 hour
Cooling 1 hour
Freezing No need, as it will keep for ages in an airtight container in the fridge

Ingredients
830ml (1½ pints) pomegranate juice
100g (3½oz) caster sugar
50ml (2fl oz) lemon juice

Method
* In a large uncovered heavy-based saucepan, heat the pomegranate juice, sugar and lemon juice on a medium-high heat or until the sugar dissolves and the juice simmers.

* Reduce the heat to maintain a simmer for about 1 hour or until the juice becomes syrupy and has reduced by about a quarter in quantity. As it cools, the juice will thicken up.

* Remove from the heat, pour into a covered container and chill in the fridge for 1 hour before using.

Tip: I use Pom Juice to make my molasses, as it is 100% pomegranate juice with no added sugar.

Dairy-free cream

A versatile cream that can be used to frost cupcakes and fill sponges. Whilst I normally flavour it with golden vanilla extract, it works equally well with flavours such as coffee and strawberry.

Makes Enough to frost 18 cupcakes or fill a
    20cm (8 inch) sponge
Preparation 10 minutes
Cooling 30 minutes + 1 hour chilling
Freezing Yes

Ingredients
25g (1oz) wheat- and gluten-free plain flour
110ml (3½fl oz) soya milk
115g (4oz) dairy-free spread
50g (2oz) icing sugar
½ tsp golden vanilla extract

Method
* Over a medium heat in a heavy-based saucepan, mix the flour and milk with a wooden spoon until it comes to a low boil and thickens into a paste. I have tried using a variety of milk replacements, but soya milk gives the best results because it is thicker and creamier (though it will work with rice or almond milk).

* Remove from the heat, place in a small bowl and cover with a damp piece of kitchen towel and clingfilm, making sure the kitchen towel comes into contact with the flour paste otherwise a skin will form. Leave to cool to room temperature for about 25 minutes. You can speed the process up by popping it in the fridge for 15 minutes.

* In a large mixing bowl, use a hand-held electric mixer to cream together the dairy-free spread, icing sugar and golden vanilla until light and fluffy. If you prefer a sweeter cream, use a little more icing sugar to taste.

* Beat in the cooled flour and soya mixture with the mixer on a high-speed setting. You need to beat at high speed for several minutes to ensure the flour mixture has been incorporated completely into the creamy mixture. Cool in the fridge until needed.

Tip: When making the cream filling, use a light-coloured vanilla extract. Dark Madagascan vanilla will make the cream too dark in colour. It is also important you cool the flour and soya milk mixture to room temperature before adding it to the dairy-free spread and icing sugar. If you don't, your cream will curdle.

Dairy-free evaporated milk

Evaporated milk is simply milk that has had about 60% of its water removed, so imagine my delight when I realized I could quickly and easily make my own using dried soya or almond milk.

Makes About 180ml (6fl oz)
Preparation 5 minutes

Ingredients
70g (2½oz) dried soya milk powder

Method
* Mix the dried soya milk powder with 140ml (5fl oz) water and stir together until smooth.
* Pour into a covered container and store in the fridge until required.

Tip: The milk can be stored in an airtight container in the fridge for up to two weeks, just stir before using.

Stockists

Cake Angels stock some of the harder-to-find ingredients such as dairy-, wheat- and gluten-free chocolate drops, dried soya milk powder, soya creams and a small selection of decorations.
www.cakeangels.co.uk

Doves Farm Foods are one of the UK's leading gluten-free and wheat-free flour specialists. Their self-raising flour recently won the Fair Trophy for the best 'free from' food of 2011. Their products, including xanthan gum, can be easily sourced at supermarkets and health food shops nationwide.
www.dovesfarm.co.uk

Goodness Direct is a mail order company where you can source a variety of specialist ingredients.
www.goodnessdirect.co.uk

Naturally Good Food is a shop based in Leicestershire providing an extensive range of specialist ingredients. They have a mail order service that is prompt and reliable.
www.naturallygoodfood.co.uk

The Vegan Store Direct is a great one-stop shop for dairy-free chocolate, milks and creams.
www.veganstore.co.uk

Cake Craft World is an online shop specializing in everything to do with cake decorating, from books to boxes and everything in between. What I like about their edible decorations are the ingredients labels. A lot of decorations contain wheat starch, so it is important to check before you order. Many companies don't know what is in the decorations they sell.
www.cakecraftworld.co.uk

Squires Kitchen is a huge online shop selling cake decorating equipment and supplies.
www.squires-shop.com

Almond Art, based in Clacton-on-Sea, Essex, stocks a wide range of decorating equipment and supplies, as well as offering specialist cake decorating courses.
www.almondart.com

Edible Glitter supplies a brilliant range of edible glitter colours, ranging from baby pastels to dark, vibrant neons.
www.edible-glitter.co.uk

Scrumptious is a company based in Ludlow, Shropshire supplying a range of sprinkles, a number of which are dairy-, wheat- and gluten-free. They also stock a good range of edible glitters, colours and muffin cases.
www.scrumptious.uk.net

Index

Acknowledgements

❧

Where to start? There are so many people I would like to thank for helping me turn a childhood dream into reality. To John and Charlie for supporting me, cheering me on, calming me down and bravely tasting every recipe put in front of them. To all my family and friends who have encouraged me in my belief that I could start a business doing something I love, you know who you are. A huge thanks to Marc and Lorraine for spending hours discussing design concepts with me and creating my special Cake Angels logo; I love it. My grateful thanks to Gareth Roberts and Chris Cook for all their hard work on turning my design ideas into actuality. Thank you to Paula Snow and Frankie and all the girls at the Hereford Breast Cancer Haven for being there when I needed you and for always being so enthusiastic about my cakes.

A special thanks to the brilliant journalist Catherine O'Brian, who wrote a wonderfully upbeat article about my battle with breast cancer and the start of Cake Angels: without that article, there wouldn't have been a book. A big thank you to Clare Hulton, my agent, who read that article, had the vision of Cake Angels the book and has guided me seamlessly and effortlessly through the literary jungle. A massive thanks to Lizzy Gray, Helen Hawksfield and the team at HarperCollins: your unfailing enthusiasm and faith in me kept me going many times late into the night! Thanks to Laura, Annie, Lisa, Rachel and Annie for the beautiful photographs and thanks to Kay for helping me to 'dot my i's and cross my t's.'

Thank you, thank you, thank you to Shirley, Dwayne, Jack and the Ebenites for keeping Charlie happy when Mummy had to work. A massive thank you to the Jackson Five, especially Anna, who was with me at the start of Cake Angels and who is always happy to spend hours talking cake!

For seven years I have been trying to think of a way to say thank you to the tirelessly hardworking Dr Sean Elyan and Mr Alan Corder and Dr Vanessa England. Without your care, expertise, patience and unfailing support, Charlie and I might not be here: thank you.

This book also gives me the opportunity to thank Professor Jane Plant, for introducing me to the benefits and joys of eating without dairy and for taking the time to talk to me and encourage me when I was scared and depressed: thank you.

Finally a huge thank you to all my wonderful customers: without you, there wouldn't be a Cake Angels.

To John and Charlie, I love you both,
Julia xx

First published in 2011 by Collins
an imprint of HarperCollins*Publishers*
77–85 Fulham Palace Road
London W6 8JB

www.harpercollins.co.uk

10 9 8 7 6 5 4 3 2 1

Photography © Laura Edwards, 2011
Text © Julia Thomas, 2011

Julia Thomas asserts her moral right to be identified as the author of this work.
A catalogue record for this book is available from the British Library.

978-0-00-743929-4

Food stylist: Annie Rigg
Props stylist: Lisa Harrison
Commissioning editor: Lizzy Gray
Project editor: Helen Hawksfield
Cover designer: Heike Schuessler
Designer: Sophie Martin

Printed and bound in Spain by Graficas Estella, S.L.